Experiences of S…

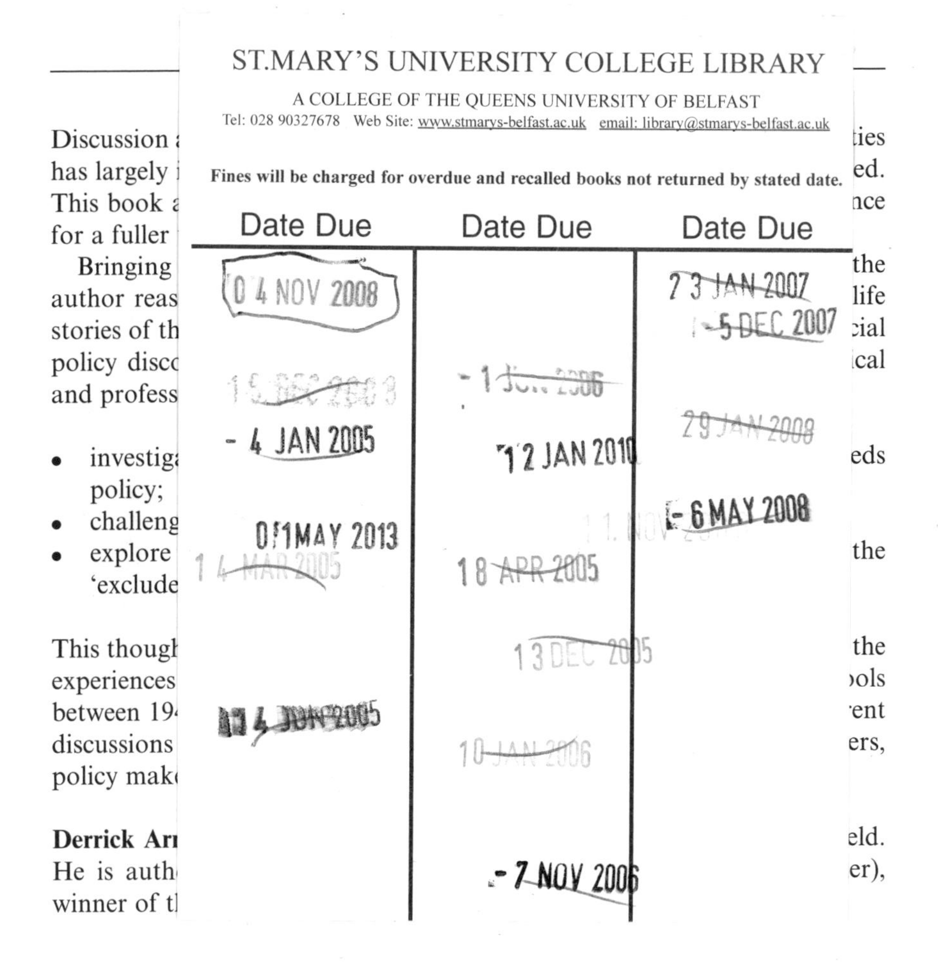

Discussion … ties
has largely … ed.
This book … nce
for a fuller …

Bringing … the
author reas… life
stories of th… cial
policy disc… cal
and profess…

- investig… eds
  policy;
- challeng…
- explore … the
  'exclude…

This though… the
experiences … ools
between 19… ent
discussions … ers,
policy mak…

Derrick Ar… …eld.
He is auth… er),
winner of t…

Experiences of Special Education

Re-evaluating policy and practice through life stories

Derrick Armstrong

RoutledgeFalmer
Taylor & Francis Group
LONDON AND NEW YORK

First published 2003
by RoutledgeFalmer
11 New Fetter Lane, London EC4P 4EE

Simultaneously published in the USA and Canada
by RoutledgeFalmer
29 West 35th Street, New York, NY 10001

RoutledgeFalmer is an imprint of the Taylor & Francis Group

Typeset in Times and Gill by BC Typesetting, Bristol
Printed and bound in Great Britain by
MPG Books Ltd, Bodmin, Cornwall

British Library Cataloguing in Publication Data
A catalogue record for this book is available from the British Library

Library of Congress Cataloging in Publication Data
A catalog record has been requested

ISBN 0–415–26614–9 (hbk)
ISBN 0–415–26615–7 (pbk)

There is a history of imaginary geographies which cast minorities, 'imperfect' people, and a list of others who are seen to pose a threat to the dominant group in society as polluting bodies or folk devils who are then located 'elsewhere'.

David Sibley, *Geographies of Exclusion*

Contents

Acknowledgements

This book arose out of research on the 'Life Histories of People with Learning Difficulties' undertaken between 1996 and 1998 with the support of the ESRC (Grant No. R000221555) and a second ESRC award between 1998 and 2000 (Grant No. R000237697) for a project on 'Self Advocacy, Citizenship and the Social Model of Disability'. I would like to thank the ESRC for their support for this work. A special debt of gratitude is owed to the participants in these projects. However, this book does not attempt to speak for them. It attempts to engage with their lives from the perspective of my own commitment to a politics of liberation. My thanks also go to Yvonne Hampton and Tim Kent who helped collect the stories told here. The ideas put forward in this book have been developed over a number of years and in discussions with many people. I would particularly like to mention my PhD students who have both stimulated and challenged my thinking: Abdelbasit Gadour, Vickie Heathcote, Tim Kent, Pippa Murray and Ilektra Spandagou. Thanks also to my colleagues at the University of Sheffield, particularly Ann Cheryl Armstrong, Felicity Armstrong, Len Barton, Wilf Carr, Peter Clough, Danny Goodley and Gary McCulloch. Finally, and not least, my family, Cheryl, Jennifer, Robert, Adam and Peter, without whose support this book could not have been completed.

A version of Chapter 2 has previously been published under the title 'Historical voices: philosophical idealism and the methodology of "voice" in the history of education', in *History of Education*, 2003, vol. 32, no. 2, pp. 215–231 and I am grateful to the editors and publishers (http://www.tandf.co.uk) for permission to include this here.

Introduction

The history of special education is for the most part a hidden history. Rarely are the voices of those who were schooled in this system heard. Yet throughout the twentieth century a significant number of children were identified as having learning difficulties and placed in segregated special schools. The 1944 Education Act introduced compulsory secondary education for all children with the exception (until 1970) of children with severe learning difficulties. The 1981 Education Act saw a development of this 'inclusive' philosophy with the abolition of categories of special educational need and an assessment policy based explicitly upon the idea of a continuum of educational need. There are important continuities in special educational policy in this period as well as some significant divergences, yet little is known about the experiences and perspectives of those who were 'included' within the special education sector as a result of these policy shifts. The proposition put forward in this book is that these 'insider' perspectives are of central importance for an understanding of special education policy during this period.

The language of special education

Special education, like other social phenomena, is the product of competing and often contradictory discourses, policies, social interests and practices. Although there are many variations and overlaps between them, three discourses in particular can be identified as having impacted in significant ways upon the development of special education. The first of these is a discourse of exclusion and segregation, which has its roots in the eugenics movement of the nineteenth and early twentieth centuries. The second is a discourse of 'normalisation', which characterised educational policy in the second half of the twentieth century. More recently a discourse of 'inclusion' has gained prominence, particularly in the critical literature on special education, but also in the rhetoric, at least, of government policy and school practices. Contradictions are to be found both within and between these discourses. For instance, following Ulrich Beck's thesis of the 'risk society',[1] the policy discourse of 'inclusion' may be seen as emanating from an alternative articulation of the 'problem' as one of 'risk management'[2] or, to put this another way, as the management of excluded populations!

The enormously powerful eugenics movement of the late nineteenth and early twentieth centuries has left a lasting influence upon educational policy. However, it was rooted in the belief that the only way to prevent mental, physical and moral contamination of the 'healthy' population was to identify and segregate those who were 'degenerate', preventing them from breeding.[3] In the second half of the twentieth century this discourse was replaced by the discourse of 'normalisation', which acknowledged the educational needs of children with learning difficulties and provided schooling opportunities, for the most part within a greatly expanded separate special school system. From the 1970s considerable interest was shown in the policies of integration and this thinking was taken up in the Warnock Committee's Report on Special Educational Needs.[4] More recently, 'inclusive' education has become an important policy discourse.

Following the 1981 Education Act there was some evidence of a reduction in segregated placements[5] but it was in the 1990s that a policy discourse began to develop around 'inclusive education', informed in particular by the experiences of disabled people and their struggles for human rights. However, running parallel to this latter discourse, the 1980s saw a significant shift in educational policy towards marketisation of educational services and an audit-based culture of accountability. The apparent dichotomy between these two perspectives has led to questioning of the 'assimilationist' objectives that seem to underpin 'inclusive' policies.[6] These contradictory discourses have provided the backdrop against which practical struggles over the meaning and purpose of educational policy have been carried out: what Gillian Fulcher has called 'enacted' policy.[7]

Whose history is this? Placing special education within its historical context

The growth of special education in the UK in the nineteenth and twentieth centuries cannot be understood in isolation from the broader context of the contested purposes and structures of the larger education system and of the latter's place within and as an agent of societal change. The aim of this book is to examine the policy discourses that have constructed 'otherness', 'assimilation', 'inclusion' and 'exclusion' through systems of special education. It will do so by exploring how the history of 'special education' has been experienced in the lives of people labelled as having 'learning difficulties', and the ways in which such labels have been internalised and resisted.

Much of the history of special education has been a 'hidden history'. The history that has been told has largely been that of the policy makers and the professionals who have constructed the edifice of special education. Thousands of voices have gone unheard in this 'official' history: in particular, the voices of those whose lives have been most affected; that is, those who were identified and categorised as being 'in need'. Felicity Armstrong has argued:

> Historical accounts which trace the development of special education only through formal policy making and its documents (i.e. education acts, policy documents) leave out the messiness, variety and unpredictability of policies as they are enacted through social practice. Social practices are socially and culturally rooted within particular political, temporal and spatial contexts. Importantly, what is going on where, who is involved and in what historical period are all crucial elements in the unravelling of social practice.[8]

It is the contention of this book that these stories bring new perspectives to an understanding of the education system and of the construction of identities in relation to social practice, social organisation and social power. Moreover, it is important that they are heard and acknowledged because, in speaking their history, people empower themselves to resist the colonisation of that history.

Porter, in a study of the writings of people labelled as 'mad', has argued that:

> the mad highlight the hypocrisies, double standards and sheer callous obliviousness of sane society. The writings of the mad challenge the discourse of the normal, challenge its right to be the objective mouthpiece of the times.[9]

The research base for this book

The focus of this book is on a particular group of people placed outside of the mainstream of society: namely, those identified as having 'learning difficulties'.[10] It is based on research carried out with forty people of different ages who had, as children, been identified as being 'mentally retarded', 'subnormal', or as having 'learning difficulties'.[11] Their ages spanned attendance at schools from the years immediately before the 1944 Education Act up until 1994 (see Table 1), and their life stories were collected over a two-year period using a variety of methods developed in collaboration with the participants themselves.

It has only been possible to report a small number of these stories in detail in this book. None the less, the other stories have played a major role in informing the argument of the book.

Table 1 Sample age and gender distribution

Schooling period	*Female*	*Male*	*Total*
← 1944–1954	4	3	7
1955–1964	3	4	7
1965–1974	2	5	7
1975–1984	4	6	10
1985 →	3	6	9
TOTAL	16	24	40

The project had 5 aims:

1 to describe the experience of special education from the perspective of people who attended special schools because of learning difficulties during the period 1944 to the present;
2 to explore how changing conceptualisations of special educational needs during this period affected the experiences of people whose schooling occurred in these contexts;
3 to consider, from the perspective of people who attended special schools because of learning difficulties, how the experience of special education has affected subsequent life opportunities;
4 to contribute to a theoretical understanding of the development of 'special needs' in educational and social policy;
5 to contribute to the development of life story methodologies in research with adults who experience learning difficulties.

Speaking for whom about whom?

Much has been written about 'voice', in recent years, particularly in respect of 'marginalised' voices. Within some parts of this literature there is a strong theme of the importance of not speaking for other people but letting voices be heard in their own words without the encumbrance of authorial interference, misrepresentation or even colonisation. There is, in my view, a lot to be said for this argument. Without being contextualised in a broader life experience, stories easily become words that can be used to say all sorts of things. But in treating history as if it can be reduced to the different stories that are told we fall into a postmodern paradox. On the one hand, the politics of difference emphasise that each story comprises a unique and valid perspective on the world. On the other hand, postmodernism recognises that through our own stories we interpret and make sense of the stories of others and in doing so turn these stories into other than what they were. If we can never have access to the untrammelled perspective of the other, it follows that we cannot act together in ways that demonstrate solidarity across differences and that the politics of difference is reduced to the politics of individualism. This is a position that I believe to be fundamentally wrong as well as divisive and disempowering.

There is a balance to be struck between empathy and analysis. In my view, this balance is struck in the practice of social life. It does not lie in the posturing identity politics of those academics who celebrate difference by closing down possibilities for engaging politically across difference and attempting to understand what is common across oppressions. In this sense, there is actually a responsibility for an author to speak and, in doing so, to make sense of social life. Of course, in doing so, one can make mistakes and of course the voice of the author can dominate in ways that are themselves oppressive. But besides responsibility there is also accountability. In this respect, the academic community has a particular responsibility of its own. This responsibility is not only to subject the work of their colleague academics to criticism but a responsibility to speak critically about the world, challenging what is taken for granted as 'normal'. It is with these thoughts in mind that this book has been written and by which it will be judged.

In writing the book it very soon became clear that a chronological history of special schooling in the post-Second World War period would not do justice to the richness of the life stories that had been given to me. These stories are about lives, not simply about schooling. At face value, the stories that were told about the experience of education were often limited, half-remembered and certainly not analytical in dissecting the impact of particular policy positions and shifts. Yet, just under the surface of their accounts of day-to-day life, both in the past and in the present, lay experiences and insights that opened up a whole new perspective on the impact (and non-impact) of special educational policy on the ways in which people understood and represented their lives. Policy cannot be adequately understood in terms of the impact of specific formulations. Rather, it enters into social practice as one form of engagement with the lives of those at whom it is directed. Its constructions and impacts unfold over time and are subject to contestation, reformulation and reconstruction within and by a wide range of competing social forces and processes. The relationship of policy to life stories therefore is one that must also be set within a theoretical and analytical context that goes beyond the specific experiences and perspectives of individuals. Individual stories, it will be argued, provide insights into the nature and operation of these forces both through the internalisation of subordination and through resistance. Such an approach allows exploration of the continuities and discontinuities of policy but it also reveals the role of policy as one, important but contested, strand in the social practice of human affairs.

Structure of the book

Chapter 1 provides an overview of the development of special education in the UK up until the 1944 Education Act. It traces the origins of modern conceptions of 'disability' and the treatment of these conditions through what Foucault has referred to as 'technologies of power'. It is argued that the eugenics movement heavily influenced the expansion of segregated special education in the late nineteenth and early twentieth centuries. Moreover, this movement has left a continuing legacy in special educational policy. However, it is also argued that a strong assimilationist policy was developing prior to 1945 which was rooted both in rationalist conceptions of humanity and in the economic demands of industrial capitalism for the efficient production and management of labour power.

Chapter 2 is concerned with the methodology of voice. It questions why the voices of people with learning difficulties have been excluded from histories of special education. It is argued that this question is in part answered by examining the role of the historian, the philosophical assumptions that underpin historical methodology and the ways in which voices are mediated through the ambiguities of authorship. This point is developed through a review of different approaches to historical authorship. An argument is presented for drawing upon the narratives of those 'insiders' whose experiences remain on the margins of documentary histories, to unpack the nature of dominance through those points of resistance that reveal the structures and processes of hegemonic and normalising social relations.

Chapters 3 to 5 examine key periods in the development of special education during the second half of the twentieth century through the life stories of participants in that system. The focus here is not simply upon schooling but upon the lives of people who began their schooling within these periods.

In Chapter 6 it is argued that the development of schooling in the twentieth century was fundamentally concerned with institutionalising social control, informed by an ideology of scientific rationalism. Many children with learning difficulties had been institutionalised before 1944, particularly in asylums for 'idiots' and 'imbeciles'. However, the educational philosophy of care, treatment and rehabilitation that dominated the post-war reform agenda led to the inclusion of many disabled children within the education system for the first time. By contrast, but equally important, agitation by teachers for the removal of 'troublesome' and 'deficient' children from the ordinary school also contributed to an expansion of the special education sector. However, it is argued that these reforms in many respects reflect the continuity of policy. From the late 1970s onwards more profound social changes began to unfold as society moved towards late modernity. These changes brought about a significant reconceptualisation of special educational needs. The chapter argues that the impact of this extended beyond special education and was concerned with reformulation of regulatory systems themselves in this period.

Chapter 7 examines the processes and resistances involved in the construction of identities in the context of special educational policy in the twentieth century. It does so through the 'hidden transcripts' of social life that create and defend social spaces of dissent.

It is often assumed that citizenship is dependent upon a concept of a person that incorporates autonomy, rationality and the faculty of making choices and entering into agreements. On this model, people identified as having learning difficulties have at different times and to different degrees been excluded from citizenship. Yet this model of citizenship ignores the way in which the stated features of citizenship are themselves socially constructed. Chapter 8 discusses the experience of citizenship in the lives of people labelled as having learning difficulties.

Finally, Chapter 9 draws together findings from this book to reassess policy objectives for an inclusive society in which differences are respected and social justice is embedded in the social relations of everyday life.

Chapter 1

The menace of the 'other' within

Introduction

Special education is a product of modernity. Its origins lay within the transformation of European societies over the last five hundred years and its social role has developed in particular over the last one hundred years. To talk about special education outside of the context of historical change during this period would be to offer only very limited insight into the problems that special education was intended to address. The problems addressed by special education are modern problems; the needs that it identifies are modern needs. The fact that so much is made today of the child's needs, as if these exist independently of a social context, speaks volumes for the way in which the norms and values of our daily experiences are constructed to rationalise and legitimate the world *as it is*. To understand special education is to unpack the social practices that construct it in one way rather than in some other way.

This chapter provides a starting point for engaging with the life stories that follow. It is concerned with contextualising the discussion within a historical framework: namely, that of the transition from modernity to late modernity. The detailed argument will be developed in subsequent chapters but the starting point for this analysis lies in the growth of special education as a regulatory structure: that is, as a system of control within society. How and why these systems arose and what their relationship is to broader areas of social transformation occurring in the late nineteenth and early twentieth centuries are the concerns of this chapter.

Early Christianity: poverty, disability and 'the quality of mercy'

Although special education is a product of modernity, systems of care for the 'disabled', the 'ill' and the 'insane' did pre-date industrialised societies. In medieval Europe, for instance, religious communities cared for the severely handicapped. The term 'cretin', which is a derivative of the French word 'chrétien' (Christian), is testimony to the integral relationship between bodily care and spiritual care in those times. Of course there is also much evidence to suggest that attitudes to life in pre-industrial societies differed in significant ways from those that are familiar today. There are certainly examples of the way in which the treatment of disabled people in pre-industrial societies would be judged harsh and inhuman by the moral 'standards' of Western Europe today (although, in practice, examples of such inhumanity abound in industrial societies too). Yet, there are also examples of the social inclusion of disabled people in pre-industrial societies, once the rigours of birth and infancy had been survived, or when impairments were acquired later in life. A lack of sentimentality about life was perhaps born out of the harsh conditions of many pre-industrial societies.

Henri-Jacques Striker[1] has argued that the significance of Christianity in relation to disability lay in its breaking of the connection between disability and individual fault. 'The practice of Jesus the Nazarene is relief and cure.'[2] Prior to the Christian revolution human beings were classified into categories of 'the pure' and 'the impure', with impurity afflicting the disabled leading to restrictions being placed upon their social participation in society. 'But in shattering the prohibition, the texts of the Gospels put the integration of the unfortunate back into the hands of ethical and spiritual conscience.'[3]

Foucault[4] describes how, in the Middle Ages, 'insanity' and 'idiocy' were a part of everyday life, and 'fools and mad men walked the streets'. Similarly, Striker argues that like the fool 'the disabled person share[d] the status of the cared for . . . under supervision the fool was admitted to ordinary life'.[5] Throughout the Middle Ages there was no clear distinction between the poor and the disabled. Disability was not the primary problem: 'it is neither inventoried, nor excluded, nor organized, nor viewed in any special way: it is simply there, part of the general human lot of misery. It too deserves mercy.'[6]

The creation of 'otherness'

The fifteenth century marked the beginning of new attitudes in Europe towards disability. A time of plague, demographic change, social dislocation and rising criminality saw the poor and the disabled becoming for the first time the object of treatment. The image of 'the ship of fools',[7] sailing in the waters between countries, always menacingly at the margins, 'symbolized a great disquiet suddenly dawning on the horizon of European culture at the end of the Middle Ages'.[8] The external threat of extinction was transformed into a 'continuous and constant form of existence',[9] 'a subtle rapport that man maintains with himself'.[10] Otherness had become a part of selfhood, not something separate and distinct from, but something that only had meaning in terms of, the self, and threateningly so as a part of that self. 'Normality' was no longer to be defined by the certainty of religious and social order but by the management of self, by the containment of desire, by the control of what was within, by security against what one might have been or might in the future become. Insanity and disability were no longer 'facts of life' which signified different elements of the same social whole, but were reconstructed within the lives of all; they were the markers, the symbols of vulnerability and social alienation that we all face. The 'ship of fools' was 'moored now, made fast among things and men. Retained and maintained. No longer a ship but a hospital.'[11] Thus the social meaning of disability was transformed, through the notion of 'treatment', into the management of self: 'in this "hospital" confinement has succeeded embarkation'.[12]

A distinction, which later was to become commonplace down to the present day, between 'deserving' and 'undeserving' poor began to surface in the contemporary writings: a distinction of 'the true poor, ill, feeble-minded, and infirm from the vagabonds, petty thieves, and idle, all healthy and able-bodied'.[13] This was a distinction which identified for the first time two kinds of marginality: 'that which challenges the social order, and that, much deeper which calls into question the organization of culture and ideology. To the former belong the robbers and rovers, to the second, the disabled and foreigners.'[14] Both of these groups represented a threat to the new social order. Those at the margins of the new order, who neither cared about its values nor were included by them, were uncontrolled and undermining of its values. Yet, the threat was not simply the external threat of thievery or invasion but an internal threat. It was a threat that reflected and parodied the value system of the new order. Thievery and invasion were both products of the new order itself; first, through displacement, impoverishment and the breakdown of traditional social bonds; but, second, because capitalism itself was based upon robbery and its consequence was an alienation of self from the social bonding of humanity. The tyranny of 'unreason', of physical and mental isolation, that 'feeblemindedness' and disability were seen as representing, reflected the tyranny of individual reason, unfettered by the controls of lien. Those on the margins confronted society with the chaos that was at its very core and threatened to consume it. The management of the chaos of individual reason required incorporation of those on the margins into the order of society. Modernity was not, and logically could not be, about exclusion. The nature of this incorporation was to be intellectual and moral. There was a need to understand and explain what was feared, as well as to control and disarm those fears.

Technologies of order and the expansion of special education in England

By the mid-nineteenth century the industrialising discipline of the factory system in much of Europe had led to the setting up of systems of surveillance and control.[15] Confinement was used not simply as a means of exclusion but rather as a means for maximising the efficacy of the labouring population and the treatment and reintroduction into the workforce of those parts of the population who were a burden on the economy. The social and cultural organisation of European societies was transformed by capitalism and with this came the confinement of the 'poor', the 'unemployed' and the 'defective' in separate institutions where the 'useless' were forced to labour for their keep. The 'great confinement' enacted the control of reason, that is the rational organisation of the production of wealth and its distribution to the wealthy, over unreason: the domination of the social order of reason.

In the nineteenth century, technologies of regulation became increasingly sophisticated, fine-tuning the discrimination of different categories to maximise the 'usefulness' and control of the 'idle' and 'defective'. Tomlinson[16] has argued that the treatment of 'subnormality' must be understood within the context of the profit motive of capitalism. Capitalism required a pool of labour that could be drawn upon to meet its own needs for maximising profit. It could not tolerate the presence in society of those who were idle and defective because not only would such people make no contribution to profit-making enterprises, but they would also be a potential drain on the state.

> Yet the preparation of a normal productive 'educated' workforce in elementary schools, was seen after 1870 to be impeded by the presence of troublesome defectives. The contradiction to be resolved for the last hundred years has been the control of a potentially troublesome group by the provision of separate institutions and schooling, while keeping the cost of such provision low, and encouraging as many of the group as possible to be productive and self-sufficient.[17]

The rise of the special school in England, and therefore of a distinct and separate system of education for children with physical or sensory impairments and/or the 'mentally handicapped' and/or the 'maladjusted', has been closely linked to the expansion of the state's role as the major educational provider. Yet the provision of state education in England has always been highly contested. It would be misleading to see the development of this system as guided by one purpose, and, likewise, special education has been developed within the context of a similar range of contested perspectives and interests. For instance, the origins of the state education system cannot be adequately explained solely by reference to the expansion of education and training opportunities in response to economic needs or demands for social reform. Alongside the 'reformist' strand in educational advocacy, the state system has also traditionally played a very significant role in maintaining distinctions of social class and gender through the hierarchies of prestige and power based upon 'ability'. Education by the state meant that the poor were to be trained to be orderly productive members of society.[18]

The apparent contradiction between these is not as great as it may at first seem. There is only a contradiction here if we understand the state and its institutions as representing a homogeneous body of interests. In practice, however, the state may be better described as 'a hegemonic compromise'.[19] What this means is that within the state there are different and sometimes contradictory interests. Moreover, in its actions, the state stands in a particular but variable historical relationship to the broader 'civil society', which itself comprises multiple interests. Although the state can rule by sheer force, this is difficult to sustain within modern societies over a protracted period. Power is more efficiently exercised through a consensus that embodies dominant social interests. It is in the struggle over hegemonic control that compromises between different social interests are made, which reconstruct contradictions as consensus in our socio-political experience. Consensus is not so much about agreement as it is about historical compromises.

The incorporation of working-class children into a system of education, codified and controlled by dominant social interests and articulated through the machinery of the state, was an outcome of enormous significance. Of course there were those who resisted the introduction of compulsory education on the grounds that it would educate the poor to oppose their masters. By contrast, there were those, like the Chartists, who advocated the expansion of compulsory education with precisely this hope in mind. At each stage of its introduction and expansion the policy of compulsory education represented an important compromise between these and other social interests.

It would be far-fetched indeed to see the introduction of a segregated system of education for disabled children and children with learning difficulties simply as the result of a humanitarian movement independent from the growth of industrial capitalism and the expansion of a state-provided education system. The development of a segregated 'special' system of education in England and Wales was, undoubtedly, influenced by both humanitarian reformers and eugenicists, yet the influence of these perspectives must be seen within the overall context of developments within the general system of education.

The expansion of education to include the children of the urbanised working class during the last two decades of the nineteenth century presented teachers and school managers for the first time with the full variety of children's needs and conditions.[20] In the 1880s, the endeavour to impose discipline in the factories had been reconstructed through the system of 'payment by results', in the new training ground of the industrial working class – the schools. This system was linked to an instructional Code based upon the assumption that children 'of ordinary health and intelligence who attend school with fair regularity' could all progress at the same rate.[21] The continued expansion of compulsory education and the regulation of teachers' work under the Code placed ever-greater pressure upon the capacity of the ordinary school system to cope.

The introduction of compulsory elementary schooling brought many children into the education system for the first time, children who had previously been excluded or who had excluded themselves. By the 1880s, the assumptions embodied in the 'Code' were increasingly challenged by the presence in school of children who did not achieve the expected standards. As one London school inspector reported at that time: 'Out of every seventy children, twenty-five were entirely ignorant, they misbehaved, learned nothing and truanted.'[22] This brought into question the 'effectiveness' of individual schools (though not, until much later, the Code itself), with negative consequences for the funding of those schools deemed to be 'failing'.

Under the regime of accountability imposed by the Code, the response to diversity was exclusion from the mainstream. However, exclusion increasingly operated within the general parameters of a cohesive system of regulated social order. The differentiation of capacities and abilities was not for the most part concerned with exclusion from society (though some groups, such as those with severe learning difficulties, were to remain outside of the rehabilitating power and therefore control of science for many years to come). The technology of science was more significantly sought to specify 'normalised' social order of reason itself. For example, in 1877, W.W. Ireland[23] suggested a twelve-fold delineation of 'idiocy' to include such sub-divisions of the ineducable child as: the 'genetous'; the 'microcephalic'; the 'eclampsic'; the 'traumatic'; the 'inflammatory'; and so on.

There was a growing preoccupation with the differentiation of mental deficiency during the latter part of the nineteenth century, originating out of concerns over the ineducability of children *in terms of the Code*.[24] In England, the Idiots Act of 1886 introduced a distinction between 'lunatics' and 'idiots', providing for the placement of 'idiots' in a registered hospital or institution. The sub-class of 'imbeciles' was recognised by the Act as a group less defective than idiots. The Royal Commission on the Feeble-minded (the Egerton Commission), set up in 1886, was to further refine the categorisation of 'idiots' and in doing so recommended a principle of differentiation that has had a major influence on policy and practice ever since. This was based upon a distinction between idiots, imbeciles, and a third group of 'high-grade defectives' or 'feeble-minded' children, with different forms of provision being seen as appropriate for these different groups. The present-day policy-practice (as distinct from legal framework) categorisation of 'learning difficulties' into 'severe', 'moderate' and 'mild' is remarkable witness to the historical continuity of educational policy in this area.

The more detailed refinement in the classification system for 'defective' children must be seen in the context of wider socio-economic and political change. The industrialisation of the economy and the attendant urbanisation of social life that characterised nineteenth-century England led to the 'discovery' of the 'mental defective'. The eugenicist drive to control defective populations in the interests of social progress was focused not simply on those who were identified as being 'defective', but on maintenance of the boundaries of social cohesion. The 'defective', in ever increasing numbers, were to be controlled, not merely excluded, and the mechanisms of control were to be but one aspect of the application of broader technologies of differentiation and control that normalised the regulatory power of reason. By the end of the 1880s, the 'feeble-minded' were regarded as an educational and economic problem, and the notion that special schooling for this group would benefit the state was one that was formally recognised by the Elementary Education (Defective and Epileptic Children) Act 1899.

Eugenics and the normalising role of education

By the beginning of the twentieth century the eugenics movement was developing an increasingly sophisticated notion of the relationship between the management of populations and the nature of social development. Thus, for instance, Goddard[25] recognised that what was seen as constituting 'mental deficiency' in society was very different at different historical periods. From this observation he deduced that it was social and economic 'progress' that revealed the deficiencies of 'moral, physical and mental degenerates', rather than it being the character of particular forms of social and economic relations in society that produced these categories. Goddard argued:

> the persons who constitute our social problems are of a type that in the past and under simpler environments have seemed responsible and able to function normally, but for whom the present environment has become too complex so that they are no longer responsible for their actions.[26]

For Goddard, the growing complexity of social life created conditions under which greater numbers of people had no 'usefulness': 'The feeble-minded person is not desirable, he is a social incumbrance [*sic*], often a burdon [*sic*] to himself. In short it were better for him and for society had he never been born.'[27]

The regulation of economic activity in factories required controlled and disciplined workers ordered by the time and space of the production process as the 'hands' of machines.

The inclusion of the children of the working classes within the compulsory education system led not only to the 'discovery' of increasing numbers of 'mentally defective' children but also to an expansion of what, up to that time, had been a very rudimentary 'special' education system, centred upon a small number of institutions for the deaf and the blind.[28] Yet the different, and to some extent contradictory, pressures that underpinned this expansion demonstrate the complexity of the policy discourses involved.

In her discussion of special education policy in the UK in the early part of the twentieth century, Sutherland[29] noted how, '[i]n the bleak economic climate prevailing after 1918', plans to introduce special schooling for all 'mentally defective' children between the ages of 7 and 17 under the Mental Deficiency Act of 1913 and the Elementary Education (Defective and Epileptic Children) Act, 1914 'came to look more and more like extravagant fantasies. Lack of money drove the Board of Education first to reappraise the role of special schools and then to cease positively to campaign for them.'[30] The irony here is that special schooling for the 'mentally defective' had been proposed as a measure to extend educational opportunities. The abandonment of this policy in the years following the First World War was justified on the grounds that improved methods of identifying educational needs and matching teaching strategies to needs made it more practical to include 'mentally defective' children within the ordinary school. The reality was that large numbers of children continued to be excluded from any form of schooling.

The return of prosperity in the 1920s was reflected in the proposals of the Wood Committee.[31] The 1913 Mental Deficiency Act had defined four categories of defect – idiots, imbeciles, feeble-minded and moral imbeciles ('defective' people with criminal propensities). The report of the Wood Committee in 1929 estimated there to be 300,000 mentally defective persons in England, giving a mean incidence of 8.56 per 1,000. In every 100 mental defectives it was estimated that there would be 5 idiots, 20 imbeciles, and 75 feeble-minded. It was further argued that existing special schools were catering for no more than one-sixth of feeble-minded children who were seen as being able to benefit from an education. Moreover, it was suggested that no proper provision was being made for an even larger number of children (some 10 per cent of the population) who did not technically meet the criteria for certification as feeble-minded. Under existing legislation this group could not be admitted to special schools because they were not mentally defective, despite their exclusion from education in the ordinary school (Board of Education and Board of Control, 1929).

The Wood Committee recommended that the certification of the feeble-minded should be abolished so that the feeble-minded and the retarded could be catered for in one comprehensive system. This recommendation reflected a fairly radical shift in thinking and a movement towards a more 'inclusive' education system. The abolition of certification would, it was believed, lead to the removal of the stigma of attendance at a special school for the feeble-minded whilst at the same time extending educational provision to a much wider group of children hitherto denied access to educational opportunities.

What was becoming more apparent from this point onwards was that the eugenicist goals of the early twentieth century were beginning to be reconstructed through the language of normalisation. Despite the radical nature of these policy proposals there remained significant points of continuity with the eugenics movement and these were to be made more explicit in the actual policy changes that took place in 1944. The common ground between eugenics and normalisation lay in the ambition of both to engineer social development through the control of 'deviant' populations. Both were fundamentally concerned with notions of 'social progress' and social and individual improvement. The programme of normalisation was to draw on the increasingly sophisticated technologies of differentiation and treatment that were being developed within the welfare professions (particularly educational psychology) to extend and focus educational provision towards what were perceived to be the 'special needs' of deviant and discarded populations. The eugenics movement had promoted a society based upon an extremely narrow view of the qualities of human life. Its technologies had been employed, however, on the margins of society, confronting the perceived threat to the rationality of social order. The principle of 'normalisation', by contrast, advocated a more inclusive approach to the distribution of educational opportunities. On the other hand, normalisation extended systems of monitoring and control to larger numbers of children and their families, as well at the same time impacting more intrusively on the lives of those who challenged the social order and those who called into question the 'organization of culture and ideology'.[32] While the growth of special education promoted and encouraged 'social inclusion' based upon educational opportunities, it paradoxically did so through structures that perpetuated the segregation and isolation of those identified as 'different'.

The new policy discourse of normalisation was articulated in the 1930s by Duncan[33] who argued that:

> Segregation of feeble-minded children into special schools and the development of a narrow curriculum based on vocational and sub-vocational lines completely different in principle from a curriculum suitable for normal children have led to a view, held in the past, that feeble-minded children have educational requirements quite different from those of normal children, and to an accent on the 'special'. . . . [However, the real problem is that of] fitting education to the differing capacities and needs of all children. The same principles are sound for all.

Yet, Duncan failed to problematise the social conditions in which differences are reconstructed as deficiencies. It is for this reason that his 'humanitarian' perspective can be understood as based upon the policy discourse of 'normalisation'. It is not the social relations of a society that are seen as creating conditions under which the label of 'mental deficiency' is given meaning. The argument put forward is rather that the role of education is to meet the individual needs of each child in such a way as to incorporate difference. This is made clear as Duncan continues:

> Economic, social and educational changes that have been taking place during the last few years have revealed mental deficiency as a problem of greater magnitude than it was at one time thought to be. People suffering from a great degree of mental defect – idiots and imbeciles – have for centuries been recognized as mental cases. Such cases, however, constitute only a small minority of the total number of mental defectives. The very great majority are the higher grade – feeble-minded – type, many of whom are of normal physical appearance. In years gone by these were not obvious, did not present any very great economic or social problem. Many of them earned a living as 'hewers of wood and drawers of water'. They helped with agricultural work or with garden work, or in factories doing unskilled manual work often requiring chiefly physical strength. In recent years mechanisation of industry and the changing nature of agriculture and horticulture in this country, due to improved world transport facilities, have resulted in a diminished and diminishing demand for unskilled labour. Dislocation of industries and the changing material needs of a population may result in a pool of unemployed labour, but a general change throughout all industry, such as mechanisation, tends to result in a pool of unemployable labour. Changing industrial conditions have thus given rise to problems of unemployment and have focused attention on the existing large number of feeble-minded and intellectually dull.[34]

Thus, Duncan's philosophy of educational inclusion is perhaps distinguishable from Goddard's only by the moral position of 'care' that is adopted towards those 'unfortunates' whose 'feeble-mindedness' has been revealed by 'social progress'. The logic of this argument is quite interesting. In the absence of any critique of what constitutes 'progress' it might be thought to follow that before too long all but the most intelligent will be useless and therefore eventually categorised as feeble-minded. The inevitability of these changes is simply assumed, but at the very least questions must be raised about the criteria being used to evaluate 'progress'.

More significantly, Duncan's rhetoric of inclusion is trapped within a series of assumptions about the social world and the nature of economic development. These assumptions led him to believe that the role of the education system was to be responsive to the different needs of children as these are 'discovered' or made apparent through the increasing complexity of industrial organisation. The adoption of 'sound' principles of teaching all children, although at face value perhaps indisputable, actually amounts to a recommendation for the 'normalisation' of those who have been excluded by the 'Economic, social and educational changes that have revealed mental deficiency'.[35] Duncan first neglected to consider ways in which the education system might itself produce needs; and, second, failed to explain how these needs might be related to the interests of other social groups (for instance, the changing role of professionals).

Sociological perspectives on the history of special education

Some authors[36] have argued that the humanitarian concerns that led to a massive expansion of separate special educational provision for those children falling into non-normative categories of need after 1944 may actually be 'an ideological rationalisation which obfuscates the educational, political and economic needs actually served by the expansion'.[37] Humanitarian perspectives see the growth of special education as reflecting concerns about the care of children whose disadvantaged lives limit their educational opportunities. Yet, those who adopt a humanitarian perspective on special needs 'still have to explain why a whole sub-section of special education has developed and expanded, which is backed by legal enforcement and caters largely for the children of the manual working class'.[38]

Elsewhere Tomlinson has argued that:

> technological advance has permanently displaced the need for manual labour. . . . Now achievements in ordinary education (which are based on reading) are crucial to gaining any kind of employment or income above subsistence level. Those who are defined as unable or unwilling to participate in ordinary education are likely to remain partially or permanently unemployed and to be destined for a life of relative dependence and – however humanitarian – of more social control. . . . However, such a society needs to rationalise the resulting 'uselessness' of many of its citizens. Special education becomes a means of legitimating a labour crisis by dealing with the 'useless'.[39]

The conceptualisation of educational failure in terms of personal deficits for which a humanitarian concern is appropriate serves to marginalise and contain opposition to structural changes in society. Humanitarian conceptualisations of 'need' legitimate the disempowerment of those identified as 'needy' by denying them the equal opportunity to negotiate a definition of their own needs in terms of their political and social origins.

An alternative account of the creation and growth of a 'special' sector of education links this directly to policies encouraging the sorting and discarding of those considered to be 'useless' in the modern world. Ford *et al.* maintained that the definition of children as 'deviant' or 'special' serves to depoliticise both their behaviour and the construction of their needs as different from those of 'normal' children.[40] Thus, the education system itself becomes a vehicle providing explanations for social and economic inequalities which legitimise that inequality.[41]

Conclusion

Policy and provision for special education are frequently cast within a framework that ignores the historical context within which it has developed. 'Inclusion', for instance, is not an abstract principle but is rather a policy discourse that is politically defined at and by specific historical moments. Medical and psychological perspectives on special education, by contrast, have tended to emphasise the individuality of need and in so doing slip into deficit theories of needs that decontextualise the relationship between having need and the power to define the needs of others. There has been a tendency to focus upon the child and his or her needs in ways that ignore how those needs have been constructed through the interplay between the education system and wider social, economic and political processes and conditions. Rather than supporting a critique of the social construction of needs, those constructions are instead legitimated. The social context within which the child is situated is treated as unproblematic. Yet, medical and psychological perspectives on special education are themselves historically located in the histories of those professions as well as in the history of social life more generally.

This chapter has argued that the growth of special education is embedded in the rationalist ideology of modern society. Policy and practice interventions have been centred upon the management of difference, either through its eradication, as with the eugenics movement, or through its 'treatment', as with the policies of normalisation. Continuity between these two policies lies in their mutual commitment to a narrow and homogeneous view of social inclusion and control within a cohesive but highly differentiated and hierarchical ordering of place, values and norms. The paradox of modernity arises from, on the one hand, the freeing of individual will as a creative vehicle for social transformation, and, on the other hand, the ordering of social life to limit the impact of diversity upon the contentment that universalises specific social interests as the natural order. It will be argued in the remaining chapters of this book that the life histories of those subordinated within this 'inclusive society' reveal the cracks in contentment that illustrate this paradox and point to the reasons for the collapse of the post-war compromise in education.

Chapter 2

Whose history is this?

Challenging 'official' narratives of educational history

Introduction

Histories of education have rarely moved far beyond the voices of official policy makers in their analysis of policy development in the field of special education. The voices of those who have made policy through government committees and reports and of those professionals who have implemented and sometimes contested these policies have been the dominant voices in the story of special education. History rarely engages with the inarticulate and 'mentally deficient'. As Ryan and Thomas have argued:

> Historical accounts of mental handicap tend to be mainly concerned with institutional and legal landmarks – the building of an asylum, the passing of Acts of Parliament. Or they deal with the deeds of great men – scientific discoveries and educational reforms. . . . Virtually nothing is known of the lives of idiots and their families. Mentally handicapped people are still hidden from history as they are from the rest of life. What history they do have is not so much theirs as the history of others acting either on their behalf, or against them.[1]

History lives through the forms of its representation. The historical text can engage with the past in ways that legitimate and reify certain perspectives and voices as well as in ways that probe and critique the authority of those voices. In one sense, this might be understood as an issue about sources and the technicalities of historical method. On the other hand, the writing of history might be understood in terms of a contested struggle for legitimacy. Certainly, the writings of historians, along with historical documents, are themselves part of a historical record. They speak to the way in which the world *is now* through constructions of the past, as well as to the way in which it was through constructions of the present.

This chapter questions the way in which the voices of people with 'learning difficulties' have been excluded from historical analyses of the policies and policy interactions that have been instrumental in the formation of their 'public' identities and their, often more private, resistance. A second, but no less important, concern is to take seriously the criticism that discussions of life history, biographical and autobiographical method are frequently:

> Silent on historical method when such a contextual perspective might have served to offset the air of narcissism which can pervade such texts.[2]

History and the 'voice' of the historian

'History', according to Oakeshott, 'is the historian's experience. It is "made" by nobody save the historian: to write history is the only way of making it.'[3] Oakeshott's claim is that in looking at an account of the past, our concern should not only be with the 'facts' that are represented but also with positioning the historian in relation to those 'facts'. Historical facts don't simply exist in an archive waiting to be identified and interpreted; they construct the present and are brought to life by the act of construction, or reasoning, that the historian engages in. In this sense, the historian's 'voice' is at the centre of history. The act of reconstruction that the historian undertakes tells us about the times in which that historian lives and about the standpoint of the historian in relation to contemporary issues. It does so because the historian is part of the present, not the past; the act of construction is an engagement of the present with itself.

A similar argument was advanced by Collingwood[4] who famously argued that the writing of history is a re-enactment of the present in the past. The values of the present are, he maintained, inextricably bound up with the way we understand the past. Therefore, historical understanding is located in the particular relationship between the historian and the past, and the historical text itself constitutes evidence of the continuing reconstruction of the past by the present. Historical writing is in this sense concerned with subjectivities and embodies the representation of partial perspectives. It is a product of the present and not simply an expression of the past. As such, it engages with the present and its concerns.

For both Oakeshott and Collingwood, history is not independent of the past; it does not simply exist in the mind of the historian. Yet, the relationship between past and present is such that this empirical reality can only have meaning through its existence and representation in the present. The reconstruction of the past is not so much a fabrication of some objective reality that could be authentically reproduced, but is rather about the construction of a new coherence in the understanding of ourselves. In this sense, the historian undertakes the analysis of the past in essentially the same way as anyone else. Historical methodology might involve greater sophistication both in technique and in the use of evidence than is the case in ordinary constructions and reconstructions of self, but it does not embody any different principles.

This 'idealist' conception of history presented an important challenge to the positivistic view of history as a chronicle of events. It rejected the assumption that the past was simply 'out there' to be gathered in and that the role of the historian was tantamount to that of an archivist, putting together information about the past like a jigsaw. A radical, anti-positivist view of history opened up the possibility for an altogether new form of engagement with the past. It brought history alive and made it relevant to the concerns of the present, allowing new ways of understanding the present and framing action for the future.

The idealist theory of history also recognised that historians construct interpretations and that it is these interpretations rather than data, or 'facts', about the world that frame an understanding of the past. In other words, history is acknowledged as fundamentally a theoretical activity in which meaning is constructed through the historian's explanations, constructions and categorisations. This is not to suggest that history can be *arbitrarily* constructed in the mind of the historian. However, it does point to the importance of the observer in putting sense into what is observed and how the ways in which the historian experiences the world through his or her social, cultural, economic, political position in it may influence what story he or she has to tell. Therefore, the focus of the historian's enquiry can be seen as at least strongly influenced by present-day concerns and interests.

Harold Silver has drawn attention to the ways in which the interests of the twentieth century help to explain the silences about the nineteenth.[5] While twentieth-century discussions of the history of education have overwhelmingly been about the system, with its implications about the interests and role of the state, historians have largely ignored the child itself and the network of relationships that constitute the child's experience. Yet these networks may provide a more meaningful context for understanding the relationship of the child to the emergent system of education in the nineteenth century, as well as suggesting an alternative framework for understanding and critiquing the growth of state-sponsored education. Silver argued that because of the twentieth-century concern with education as a *system*: 'The underlying pattern . . . is one of neglect of questions relating to educational realities, to the impact of education, to its role in cultural and social processes.'[6]

The focus of historical enquiry has been upon policy and policy makers rather than upon the experience and resistance of those participating in education, as pupils, as parents or as teachers. Precisely because the methodological implications of the historian's own values, interests and experiences are so rarely considered as important, let alone problematised, a form of ahistoricism is adopted. This ahistoricism not only restricts an understanding of the past to the concerns of the present but also ignores the complicated and diverse contexts within which policy operates. There has been a tendency to see the growth of education systems unidimensionally, either as a system of control and regulation or as a vehicle for advancing social reform and new opportunities for the mass of the population.

Yet, as Stephen Ball has argued, policies:

> are representations which are encoded in complex ways (via struggles, compromises, authoritative public interpretations and reinterpretations) and decoded in complex ways (via actors' interpretations and meanings in relation to their history, experiences, skills, resources and context). . . . [Yet] only certain influences and agendas are recognized as legitimate.[7]

When considering the history of education it is important that we ask the question: 'Whose history is being talked about?' If we ask 'whose history?' we start to realise that history is not simply a set of facts about the world but is rather a set of contested perspectives. Secondly, it becomes apparent that some of those perspectives or voices are left out of official or dominant representations of the story altogether.

The stories of insiders emphasise the importance of contextualising education policy within the much broader arena of social policy negotiations and impacts. Taken in isolation from the way in which needs and identities are constructed in the broader historically situated social relations of particular societies, a policy agenda of 'inclusion', for instance, may be continually reconstituted, or rediscovered, in new forms but with essentially the same substantive limitations. The stories of those who have experienced special education illustrate the complex ways in which this experience is tied into the construction and management of 'uselessness'.

For example, there is clear evidence that many disabled children were left in institutions by their families.[8] Historians of special education have often drawn the conclusion from this evidence that families were happy to get rid of their disabled children. Such a conclusion is all the easier to make as it colludes with the predominant ideology that disabled children, particularly disabled children with learning difficulties, are of less value than non-disabled children.[9]

History and the social construction of 'voice'

One attempt to address the problem of excluded voices is to be found in the Pragmatist philosophy of Pierce, James and Dewey, and in those sociological and psychological theories about the construction of everyday understandings and action which take Pragmatism as their philosophical starting point. For the Pragmatist philosophers, experience is the basis of any knowledge that we can have of the world. Experience is made up of those shared understandings and meanings by which groups of people are able to make collective sense of the world and which allow them to act in the world in ways that are meaningful and effective. Dewey,[10] in particular, and later the symbolic interactionists[11] took this argument further, arguing that experience should not be understood simply as something personal; experience is characterised as social. It is the social construction of experience that gives meaning to individual experiences; meaning is shared and constructed within the context of this sharing. Our ideas about the world are constructed in relation to experiences that are centrally located within the context of social interaction.

Moreover, some ideas 'work' in that the actions which follow from them are successful whilst others do not and are rejected. Thus, our 'knowledge' of the world is not 'absolute' but rather a practical knowledge. The distinction between what is subjective and what is objective is made within experience. The world is experienced as objective because it is shared. It becomes subjective only to the extent that we are prevented from achieving our goals. The problem of relativism is overcome by the practices through which our experience reconstructs meaning in ways that allow us to achieve our goals or by informing the reconstruction of our goals to match our experience.

The validity of meaning, for the symbolic interactionists, depends upon the possibility of one social actor putting him or herself into 'the role of the other': that is, into the position of other people with whom that person shares the same experience. Meaning within these social interactions may be highly contestable, but what is of central importance is that different people are able to relate to each other in agreeing, contesting and negotiating meaning precisely because they can step outside their own particular belief systems, values and interpretations of events, to see these as others see them. This possibility provides the basis for rational behaviour and therefore for establishing criteria (which may themselves be individually contestable) which can then be used to establish the validity of particular interpretations and understandings. The very fact that such criteria are contestable in this sense provides evidence for their rational basis. There may be significant differences between perspectives but the nature of social interaction itself provides the rational structures for the mediation and resolution of different interpretations. People may choose not to value the perspective of another person but the incommensurability of perspectives is not supported by the practical logic of day-to-day social life.

It might be argued that this implies the possibility of a more radical form of Pragmatism in which analysis is focused not upon 'what works' but upon comprehending the social, political, cultural and epistemological practices through which meaning is created. On the other hand, the under-theorising of the conditions within which the negotiation of inter-subjectivities becomes formalised by, and transformed through, social structures, leaves this version of Pragmatism with little theoretical purchase with which to extend historical analysis beyond a reductionist focus on social interaction.

For this reason, radical Pragmatism finds itself easily subverted by the more conservative neo-pragmatism of Richard Rorty.[12] For Rorty, relativism remains a core concept precisely because of the difficulty in specifying non-relatively who *we* are in relation to the pragmatic solution that knowledge is constituted by *what works for us*. He argues that action can only be understood within the confines of an interpretative community; therefore, its meanings and outcomes are bound to break down when taken outside these isolated domains.[13] Rorty's relativism implies incommensurability between what works for one individual, group or community and what works for another. This claim provides a basis for rejecting universalism in history as well as in philosophy. Ironically, however, this philosophical relativism leads to a very different form of universalism: namely, the universalisation of the social, cultural and political perspective of the powerful over the less powerful. In this respect, neo-pragmatism has affinities with Nietzsche's philosophy of 'the will'.[14]

The implications of this for historical analysis are: (1) different historians are necessarily trapped within their own subjective interpretative communities; (2) there are no 'knowledge' criteria for arbitrating between what works for one and what works for another; (3) what goes by the name of 'knowledge' is constituted by those social practices that empower the 'knowledge' of some over the 'knowledge' of others. What works is what can be enforced.

This interactionist perspective on meaning gave rise to an empirical sociology that was grounded in the methodology of 'voice'. Examples of this ethnographic work included Becker's[15] study of deviance, Goffman's[16] study of asylums, Whyte's[17] study of 'street corner society', and many more. The influence of this perspective upon historical scholarship has been far less. The pragmatist/interactionist perspective could be seen as one that is focused entirely upon the present because of its concern with the construction of meaning as a product of human interaction. Despite this, interactionism does have historicist implications. Although past events are not seen as causing present action, the parameters of possible action in any situation are none the less developed historically.[18] History has significance and meaning in so far as social actors themselves construe their interactions within the framework of particular historical understandings. Moreover, history can be understood as the analysis and critique of negotiated meanings and practices. Thus, as with the idealism of Oakeshott and Collingwood, the present is all-important to any possible understanding of the past.

Copeland's neo-pragmatist comparison of the emergence of the first special classes for 'backward' children in England in the period 1870 to 1914 with the outcomes of the 1981 Education Act illustrates this point.[19] Copeland argues that special education offered a practical solution to the situation that confronted, in the one case, the local Boards of Education, and in the other, local education authorities. Arising from the 'laxity or inadequacy of national policies', he suggests that professionals and administrators operating within local authorities found the space to create significant variations in local policy as a pragmatic response to the situations they encountered. On this account, no single professional discourse dominated or even informed decision-making. The driving force of action was simply the need for practical solutions.

Copeland, following Gillian Fulcher's model of 'policy as struggle',[20] sees educational decision-making as a social practice and within this analytical framework identifies how professionals were able to empower themselves in their role as 'street level bureaucrats'[21] by negotiating policy outcomes. Developments in the history of special education are seen as the outcome of negotiations by educational administrators. Multiple and contradictory outcomes were arrived at because professional identities were independent of any particular discourse of educational need. By contrast, the contested purposes and outcomes of educational practice are neither contextualised with reference to the broader social relations of society, nor problematised in relation to the changing nature and role of professionalism in the period between 1870 and 1981.

What is most notably absent from Copeland's comparison is any analysis of the impact of the rapid growth of special educational provision in the post-1945 period and the linkages between this growth and the creation of the welfare state as an expression of solidarity among citizens and the desire for rehabilitation in post-war Europe. The 1981 legislation may have empowered 'street level bureaucrats', but of greater importance was the retreat from post-war welfare policies that this legislation symbolised, despite its rhetoric of integration. Copeland's analysis of continuity in policy simply ignores the massive discontinuity between the post-war period and what went before and came after. In consequence, we are left with a fairly superficial account of the continuities that are to be found in educational policy.

The specific example that Copeland advances to illustrate his Pragmatist theory of history is one that more fundamentally illustrates the problems that arise from a reductionist focus on interaction. It does not have the analytical tools available to it to go beyond an appreciation of the practicalities of 'what works' to explore how these workings are constructed within a wider societal context of social experience and social action. What works is understood in no other terms than the practicalities of what is enforced. Thus, Pragmatism leaves historical understanding still trapped in the ideological restrictions of present-day concerns.

'Post-structuralism in historical explanation

Neo-pragmatism also has resonance in postmodernist and post-structuralist theories. The representation of history as negotiated symbolic orders, with its attendant implication that the only meaningful history is the history of 'voice', has clear links to post-structuralist theorising on discursive practices. Similarly, Rorty's rejection of foundationalism and the possibility of knowledge bears a close affinity to postmodernist relativism.

Post-structuralist analysis, heavily influenced by Foucault, has challenged many of the assumptions underpinning previous historical scholarship and has emphasised the importance of a historical methodology that places the exploration of power and voice at its centre. As with the neo-pragmatists, knowledge practices are the focus of Foucault's analysis, but rather than trying to understand their constitution Foucault's concern is with their effects.[22] To understand how power works, Foucault maintained, is to look at the knowledge, self-understandings and struggles of those whom powerful groups in society have cast off as 'the other'.[23]

Foucault looked at the ways in which knowledge is made and remade as a cultural practice of regulation rather than trying to resolve the 'unsolvable' epistemological problem of 'what can be known about the world?'[24] Thus, he conceptualised knowledge as comprising those cultural practices through which identities and understandings are produced. Instead of being represented as an object of the understanding, knowledge becomes for Foucault a form of cultural regulation through which order is imposed within societies. It governs by the way in which options are presented, problems defined and solutions considered. What constitutes knowledge in any particular situation is seen as relative to the cultural standpoint of those who employ the concept.

This way of understanding the role of knowledge as those cultural practices that regulate and order social life has significant methodological implications for historians. In the first place, from a Foucauldian perspective history cannot be adequately represented chronologically as a series of unfolding events. The relationship between past and present is understood, as it was by Oakeshott, to be intricate. The role of the cultural historian then becomes not that of representing the temporal unfolding of historical events but rather that of delineating those practices through which knowledge is made and remade.

A second major consequence of Foucault's analysis is the decentring of the individual as a historical agent. It is argued[25] that temporal accounts of history privilege the role of social actors as the dynamic of change. Social history has largely been concerned with 'theories of action' (and actors) rather than with the ways in which cultural practices are, themselves, produced and continually remade through the discourse of knowledge. In placing emphasis upon social actors, traditional histories have been underpinned by a phenomenological epistemology of individual consciousness that is represented as being at the centre of historical action.[26] Yet, the idea of an a priori actor itself represented a radical departure during the Enlightenment in which the 'locus of truth' was transferred from a 'divine subject' to the 'human creative subject'. This historical moment has been elevated by Enlightenment historians into a scientific law of history.[27]

For Foucault, it was the discourse of knowledge as cultural practice that constructed the individuality of Enlightenment philosophy rather than the conscious actions of individuals. The shifting discourse of knowledge both made and enclosed the possibilities for action. For this reason, the centring of the individual in history is itself a partial truth, a truth grounded in the making of knowledge as a cultural process. To decentre the subject in history is to contextualise agency within the cultural practices that constitute it in its different forms and make and remake the objects of action.

The third significant shift that this perspective entails is away from an understanding of power as something that is simply held and exerted by one (dominant) group over other (subordinate) groups. Marxist approaches to educational history, in particular, it is argued, have focused upon the regulatory role of education as a function of social interests. This has led to a one-dimensional representation of power and has ignored the subtlety by which power operates through the cultural practices of knowledge production, embedded in day-to-day life.

As an alternative to that form of historicism which premises historical analysis upon a constantly unfolding progress and upon the philosophical (as distinct from historical) privileging of the individual actor as the agent of change, Popkewitz *et al.* argue that history can be reconceptualised as:

> the study of the historically constructed ways of reason that frame, discipline, and order our action and participation in the world. The purpose of the investigation into systems of knowledge (or the rule of reason) is to understand how the 'common senses' of social and cultural life are invented and *make* the objects of the action that order the possibilities of innovation and change.[28]

Recent work on 'cultural history' illustrates the way in which a focus upon the exploration of diverse voices has taken forward the mantle of idealism within educational history. Traditional historical studies are criticised for their focus upon the movement in time of events and actors, without attention being paid to how 'knowledge frames and produces its acting subjects'.[29] By examining the history of education from a 'cultural practices' perspective, which explores the ways in which practice is constructed through the interplay of competing discourses, it is argued that a serious challenge is presented to oversimplified and crudely deterministic theories. These, it is argued, position individual actions as a function of the social groups to which those individuals belong (e.g. as members of a state bureaucracy), which themselves are understood as the vehicle through which the interests of a dominant social class are pursued. Power is equated with 'ways of knowing' rather than with the interests of any particular group.

An example of this approach to historical analysis is found in Franklin's work on the growth of special classes for troublesome children in early twentieth-century America.[30] Franklin's argument is that special classes were not simply a mechanism for dealing with troublesome children. The growth of special classes in the United States school system had provided school administrators with a way of maintaining 'their historic commitment to the common universal ideal of school accessibility', at a time when this was being challenged by growing pupil numbers and diversity, including the increasing number of 'troublesome' children within the school system.[31]

Thus, it is argued, school administrators should not be seen as simply embodying narrow social interests, even though the establishment of special education did provide these administrators with 'a professional ideology that celebrated their technical expertise'.[32] More importantly, a fundamental shift towards a medicalised discourse about deviance from the mid-eighteenth century onwards provided the conditions in which schools were able to assume responsibility for the kind of children placed in special education. This discourse, like all discourses, embodies relations of power, or techniques of regulation. However, because the medicalised discourse is not simply an expression of the dominance of one group over others, it is not straightforwardly exclusionary. The medicalised discourse operates as a regulatory discourse through the normalising subjectivity of 'common schooling' or, in the language of current policy/practice, 'inclusion'.

Whereas theories of social interest have tended to see the growth of special education as the product of professional interests in defining and categorising difference (i.e. an epistemology of difference), the crucial and radical insight that the cultural histories perspective has offered is into the role of special education as a 'normalising' discourse within the historical development of the wider education system. Franklin's analysis is extremely important, deconstructing, as it does, the complex and intricate factors pertaining to the development of special education in the USA. Yet, in terms of its theoretical and methodological claims, there are four areas in which I would argue that this post-structuralist perspective on history remains problematic.

In the first place, a focus upon the discourse of knowledge (in this case, the medicalised discourse of 'deviance') tells us very little about the relationship between medicalised discourse as cultural processes and the *social structure* within which they were located. The establishment of special education not only provided administrators with 'a professional ideology that celebrated their technical expertise', as Franklin argues, but it might also be argued that it was through the incorporation of the interests of this professional middle class into the state bureaucracy that the conditions were created under which those professional interests flourished.

A second response to Franklin might focus on the far-reaching assumptions he makes about how the literature on 'social interests' has invested these with a supposed homogeneity, and further how this literature has represented the relationship between 'interest' and 'action'. His argument implies that regulation theory is premised on a notion that people pursue their 'objective' social interests irrespective of the ways in which knowledge systems impact upon and remake social life. It assumes also that such theories entail social interests that can simply be read off from a person's social position. In other words, it assumes a fairly crude correspondence theory of the relationship between social interests and social action. In spite of offering important empirical insights into the complex processes involved in the development of special education programmes in the USA, Franklin could be accused of setting up a simplistic and deterministic form of regulation theory as a straw man that is then easily demolished.

Gramsci firmly rejected determinist arguments about the relationship between social interests and social action,[33] arguing that social order was in fact constructed as a hegemonic outcome, 'negotiated' between those with different social interests. Power is embedded in these negotiations both in the sense of being used coercively to pursue particular outcomes (political domination) and in the sense of being formed through socio-cultural, as well as socio-economic and political, interactions in which the values and interests of one group are incorporated by another. Thus the existence of different perspectives on special education within the state should come as no surprise.

From a Marxist perspective, therefore, school administrators should not be understood as having homogeneous interests, or as simplistically articulating the interests of a capitalist class. The critical point here is that, for Marx, power is understood as a mediative relationship between social interests rather than as something that is simply imposed by one group and accepted by another. Thus, there is a necessary ambiguity to the character of social action. It is not simply determined externally as the product of social structure but is rather the outcome of mediated social engagements. It is formed, reproduced and transformed in the struggles that take place between different social interests to define what is common, normal and acceptable.[34]

A third problematic area for the post-structuralist account is that it does not follow from a 'social interests' perspective that special education programmes are necessarily regulatory, in the sense of being imposed on one group by another. Foucault's analysis of the regulatory character of knowledge is useful here but it does not lead inevitably to the rejection of a structural account of power. Whether or not social interests operate in this way in any given context is an empirical question that is historically situated. In the privileging of discourse over structure, the assumption is that the origins of particular forms of social organisation, systems of economic production and distribution, together with institutional mechanisms for reproducing knowledge and power as social commodities, are to be accounted for, as Nietzsche[35] would have it, as arbitrary outcomes of our sense-making.

This relativist outcome is perhaps the most serious consequence of the reductionism implicit in the post-structuralist analysis. It means that there can be no way of determining the validity of knowledge, except in terms of the power of one 'knowledge practice' over another. In this respect post-structuralism bears more similarity with the conservative, Rortian version of neo-pragmatism than with the more radical version of the symbolic interactionists. Thus, any attempt to discern underlying categories of analysis must collapse into a reductionist focus on the multiplicity of voices.

The pluralism that follows from this seriously weakens the critical capacity of historical writing. Moreover, the idea embedded in this relativist pluralism that history cannot be adequately represented chronologically, far from liberating the histories of the powerless, may be seen as further delegitimating those histories. The incommensurability between histories is resolved in practice by the power of one group to impose its view of history on to the lives of others. There is no rational basis for privileging alternative interpretations of history, and similarly no practical-political basis, if we are to follow the post-structuralist path. Furthermore, the denial of chronology is not only to deny the past of those who have been oppressed but also to deny them a future. People who don't know where they come from don't know where they are going. This is the story of the anthropology of 'primitive' peoples. It was taken for granted that 'primitive' peoples had no chronological history and that the only value they had lay in the ways in which their cultural difference illuminated 'first world' cultural superiority.

Contested histories and methodological constructions

Methodologies that incorporate life-historical approaches come in many forms. For instance, naturalist oral histories are written in such a way as to give readers the impression that they are observing the scene as described, with the implication that what is provided is an accurate reproduction of the events described or the account given by the informant.[36] Yet, the researcher's involvement in the oral history interview is itself inevitably a contributing factor to the story told. In this lies the methodological significance of Blumer's observation that meaning is always negotiated and reconstructed through social interactions.[37] The interview is a mediating social interaction through which the meaning of previous experience (of both informant and researcher) is reconstructed. Moreover, the interpretation that the researcher places upon information gathered is located within an expository framework that may only be implicit but which forms a crucial element of the account.

Dissatisfaction with naturalistic oral histories and ethnographies and their tendency to privilege the 'hidden voice' of authorship has led to alternative, experimental approaches. Alternative, experimental approaches grounded in post-structuralist historiography have tried to decentre the researcher by creating texts that are multi-layered and multi-voiced.[38] The focus of these alternative narrative approaches is on deconstructing the rhetorical devices through which 'reality' is produced.[39] Text is seen as always and necessarily a literary representation constructed through rhetorical strategies, with those strategies themselves contributing to discourses of power and resistance. It is for this reason that one of the strategies of deconstruction employed by oral historians and ethnographers has been the autobiographical reflection that McCulloch and Richardson refer to as an 'air of narcissism'.[40] The deconstruction by the author of his or her own text and its biographical location provides, from a post-structuralist perspective, the account of historical methodology that McCulloch and Richardson claim is absent.

Yet, alternative forms of representation do not remove the issue of power from the text.[41] Texts are still authored, and those alternative forms through which 'voices' are represented themselves emphasise the power of authorship every bit as strongly as naturalistic writing. Authors make decisions about their texts, including decisions about alternative forms of representation. By seeking to negate or reduce the power of the author through rhetorical strategies there is every likelihood that the alternative form of representation will simply mystify the power of the author over the text. The problem here lies more with the lack of explicitness about authorship than with any failure to democratise authorship. Indeed one could go further and argue that such rhetorical strategies reflect a confusion of theory and practice that arises directly from the subordination of social action to discourse as text. For example, forms of 'collaborative authorship' that focus upon empowering marginalised 'voices' in the text are a fiction. They rest on the false assumptions that 'voice' equates with power and that neutralising authorship is an empowering strategy for those whose voices have previously gone unheard.

The discourse of 'voice' has come in for further criticism on the grounds that in its concern with the subjectivities of experience little attention is paid to structural level concerns such as social stratification. Moore and Muller argue that this leads to a situation in which:

> voice discourse promotes a methodology in which the explication of a method's social location precludes the need to examine the content of its data as grounds for valid explanation. Who says it is what counts and not what is said.[42]

Moore and Muller are particularly critical of the way in which these 'standpoint' approaches appear to advocate progressive moral and political arguments whilst in fact conflating these with arguments that deny the very possibility of founding such values upon rational principles. In consequence, they present a relativistic challenge to any attempt to develop 'epistemologically grounded classifications of knowledge'. Post-structuralism critiques the notion of totalising epistemologies but replaces these with its own totalising methodology. This methodology collapses all categories of analysis into the discourses of knowledge production: in other words, into a reductionist focus on 'voice'. Deconstructing power is then about the deconstruction of 'voice' and the way in which power is made and remade through this discourse or that, this voice or that. To avoid the reductionism, and therefore the methodological fragmentation, of 'voice', the concept of 'power' is transformed into a metaphysical relation. Evidence can only exist in the form of the multiplicity of discourses or voices that make and remake knowledge, yet the deconstruction of each discourse reveals more voices and yet more voices, each with its own subjectivity, each with its own unique position in the world.

A significant outcome of the post-structuralist focus on what are claimed to be 'marginalised voices' is a fragmentation of the 'voices' it seeks to represent, leading to political and moral atrophy. The development of theoretical categories of analysis that might give rise to a unifying focus upon the commonalities of oppression and resistance is lost in the playfulness of anti-realist deconstruction. A significant, and ironic, consequence of this is that the representation of difference itself becomes a form of 'normalisation' in which the delineation of difference is reconstructed in descriptions of the 'exotic'. The practical implication of this model is a disintegration of resistance. Resistance is formed, broken up and reformed in ways that are arbitrarily defined. The multi-layered character of 'voice' condemns the struggle of the oppressed to the margins of social experience, and as such leads to a new conservative historicism that in celebrating difference 'renders the social agent politically innocuous'.[43] The issue that confronts a critical history that endeavours to engage seriously with the concept of 'voice' is that of how to acknowledge the 'embeddedness and contingency [of the human subject] in present political and historical conditions without, however, relinquishing the struggle against domination and oppression and the fight for social justice and emancipation'.[44]

Towards a critical history of voice

A useful distinction can perhaps be made between life stories and the methodology of life history, with the latter locating life stories within a broader framework of historical and policy analysis.[45] According to Goodson and Sikes, 'without contextual commentary on issues of time and space, life stories remain uncoupled from the condition of their social construction'.[46] Thus, the authenticity of the informant's life story is recognised, as is the significance of these stories for opening up new understandings of policy processes. However, it is also acknowledged that the subjectivity of individual experience imposes constraints that confine the perceptions of those involved within the boundaries of their own stories.

Such an approach, far from decentring the author, actually reasserts the power of the author. The author is positioned theoretically, ethically and socially, not simply through the subjectivities of the author's autobiography but at the intersection of that autobiography and society. For Goodson and Sikes, this positioning of the historian creates a dilemma. Although they hold to the need for providing historical contexts for reading life stories they are also conscious that the move from life story to life history has within it a danger in that 'it offers the researcher considerable "colonizing" power to "locate" the life story with all its inevitable selections, shifts and silences'.[47]

This ambiguity is, I would agree, unsatisfactory, but it stems not from any inherent problem with narrative approaches to history but from confusion between epistemological and ethical concerns. As with any historical story, the life-history narrative is in major part rooted in the author's understanding and representation of the past. The notion of 'colonization', as it is used in the passage quoted, places a particular interpretation upon the ethical relationships involved in the acquisition and use of stories. The ethical dimensions of methodology are clearly important and the use to which information given by one person to another can be put is contestable. Yet, this ethical statement about 'colonization' privileges a post-structuralist, relativist epistemology. It assumes that the voice of authorship is the medium through which power is reproduced. If this were the case, any explanation that draws on the voices of others would not only be ethically dubious but would also carry the epistemological consequence that there should be an equal weighting of all voices, that is a silencing of the voice of the author.

C. Wright Mills, by contrast, argued that the aim of social analysis is to 'grasp history and biography and the relations between the two within society'.[48] The validity of the author's positioning is constructed within the everyday world of social practice, but most significantly it is also tested within that experience. Similarly, from the critical realist perspective of Bhaskar, the methodological imperative lies not only in the making of connections between life stories and the historical contexts within which those stories are located, but also in the making of connections between such knowledge and the biography of the historian as a situated social actor. Historical research is not a set of procedures for detached observation and unsituated reflections, nor is it an 'arbitrary outcome' of 'sense making'. Moreover, the goal of life-historical research in education must surely go beyond simplistic and epistemologically ambiguous notions of 'voice giving' to participants. The strength of life history as a methodology lies not in the celebratory form of 'voice giving' proposed by postmodernist theorists, but in its value as a tool for critically examining the structures, operations and contestations of power in educational policy and practice through an exploration of the multiple contexts which make up the lives of participants in those systems.[49]

The exploration of individual stories does not imply that individuals can be seen as self-contained, nor should it lead historians to minimise the impact of determining structures which, in the last instance, ensure subordination.[50] However, as Judith Okely argues, it is through the very atypicality of individuals, marginalised groups, and apparently incidental moments that critical, alternative, perspectives on power are offered.[51] Life-history research and its focus on individual stories challenges the homogeneity of experience and resistance and in doing so challenges the relations of power that structurally construct 'otherness' into categories of oppression. It does so because these individuals are defined as 'other' by the structures which they resist. Thus, these voices 'both challenge the centre and show its form'. 'Through careful examination and in the telling, we can discover that specific moments in individual lives inform us about both dominance and points of resistance.'[52] The significance of these acts of resistance, Okely maintains, lies not in their demonstration of empowerment and absence of subordination. After all, a lack of subservience does not equal the absence of subordination, and activity should not be confused with equality. Rather, resistance reveals 'the cracks in contentment' through an analysis that allows the practices to be contextualised historically in specific structures of subordination and the formation of social relations. The exploration of historical narratives is concerned with unpacking the operation of those structures upon and through the narrative.

This approach to the analysis of voice in educational history suggests how a critical history can be advanced in which the life stories, particularly but not exclusively, of those whose voices have been ignored by traditional histories can be drawn upon to unpack the construction of a hegemonic social order. Methodologically it provides a basis for drawing upon oral history methods as part of a wider historical analysis of social and political legitimacy. In doing so it also frees the analysis of 'voice' from a conservative, postmodernist dissolution of social action into a politics of 'difference'. Crucially, it reframes an understanding of 'voice' in historical studies away from an empowerment stance in respect of subjectivities by emphasising the objective conditions for action and theorising the structures through which hegemonic and normalising social relations are constructed, resisted, and sometimes transformed in the lives of those whose voices are so often hidden from history.

Conclusion

I have argued that at the centre of debates concerning the place of 'voice' in historical research there is a series of methodological problems arising from philosophical idealism in the history of education. It should be clear that these concerns are not confined to narrative approaches, but it is in this field of enquiry that the methodological problem of 'voice' has emerged most strongly and has generated most anxiety.

The Pragmatist critique of positivism that pioneered research into experience as a socially constructed phenomenon was important in that it provided a model for deconstructing the processes by which social meaning is arrived at as a basis for action. I have argued that despite the many strengths of this perspective in overcoming difficulties found in traditional idealist philosophies of history its emphasis upon the phenomenology of social life leads to serious problems in (a) theorising the significance of the construction of action historically, (b) theorising social structure, and (c) accounting for the relationship between structure and agency. In addition, Pragmatism has come under attack for its assumptions about the undifferentiated character of social life. This has led to an explicitly relativist version of Pragmatism in which differences between 'interpretative communities' are seen as incommensurable, with the consequence that political power becomes the arbiter of difference. A second neo-pragmatist strand has focused attention on how power is negotiated through meanings. This version of neo-pragmatism has close affinities with the post-structuralist emphasis on power as a discursive practice.

The deconstruction of 'voice' has been central to post-structuralist theorising. This has encouraged a view of educational history as a politicised cultural practice concerned with the making and remaking of power/knowledge discourses. This view of the importance of 'voice' in educational history has a radical dimension in so far as it places critical readings of the construction of texts at its centre. It demands a critical reading of the historical text (the subjectivity of the historian) from the perspective of multiple subjectivities. Similarly, these different subjectivities, as discursive practices, embody, it is suggested, forms of resistance to orthodoxy.

None the less, I have argued that various difficulties arise from this post-structuralist perspective on historical research and that in particular it is characterised by a form of relativism that has politically conservative implications. What is absent from both the Pragmatist and post-structuralist perspectives on history is an adequate account of the historically contingent character of social action, which in turn leads the historian to focus on the methodological reductionism of 'voice giving'. The deconstruction of authorship by the 'rhetorical device' of representing multiple voices within a single text has encouraged, what Sartre might have called, 'bad faith' in historical scholarship.[53] The counter-argument has been put forward that the use of life-historical research as a methodology in the history of education should not be primarily concerned with illuminating small-scale events, but rather with the theorisation, historically, of the relationships between structure and agency, policy and experience, power and resistance, etc. In this sense, the 'voice' of authorship must be sharpened rather than blunted. This means that the historian must be concerned with unpacking the social spaces of dissent that have been created by those who resist and challenge what is imposed on them through acts of power. It is in this respect that a critical realist methodology is important because its focus is not upon exploring difference in its own right but is instead concerned with the ways in which different experiences of, and perspectives towards, education provide tools for challenging the legitimacy of structures of subordination. Methodologically, this can only be achieved by positioning oneself reflectively and critically at that intersection of biography and history.

Chapter 3

Lives in special education

Disciplinary transitions

Introduction

There are no clear figures on the numbers of children who might have been deemed to have 'learning difficulties' before the 1944 educational reforms led to a new system of special educational provision. However, in 1929 the Wood Committee[1] had estimated that no more than one-sixth of educable feeble-minded children were actually attending special schools and that the numbers meeting the criteria of feeble-mindedness (and therefore eligible for placement in special schools at that time) were only a fraction of the actual number who might benefit from special schooling. It is certainly the case that many children with severe learning difficulties received no schooling at all. It is also apparent that many children entering the ordinary school system would not be defined as having learning difficulties until later in their lives when an expanding apparatus of professional decision-making and institutional care drew in many new clients.

This chapter examines experiences of schooling for those defined, either at that time or later, as having 'learning difficulties'. It does so through the eyes of five people whose lives were fashioned in this period. Alice was institutionalised from an early age. Gertrude never attended school at all. Jim attended an ordinary school until poverty forced him into a 'special school for the poor', and subsequently into institutionalised provision for adults with 'learning difficulties'. Bernard and Beryl both attended ordinary schools but were subsequently, as adults, institutionalised because of their 'learning difficulties'.

In recent years much interesting work has been done to uncover the experiences of people, both children and adults, who were incarcerated in residential institutions for the mentally retarded in the early part of the twentieth century.[2] Many children were 'handed over' to residential institutions and in some cases they spent the remainder of their lives there.[3] These bleak places, graphically described by Atkinson *et al.* in their book *Forgotten Lives*,[4] were isolated from mainstream society. Yet, as the Wood Report indicates, a great many more children who might today have been assessed as having special educational needs continued to live with their families.[5] Of these, some certainly received no education whatever, but most attended their local elementary school.

What is apparent in all the life stories told in this chapter is that decisions about children's education were frequently made by professionals on the basis of views on the viability and quality of family life. Children with special educational needs might receive very little education within their ordinary schools and classrooms and might often be internally excluded. However, the absence of alternative provision meant that they were unlikely to be removed from the elementary school system unless their needs were judged 'severe' or their families, for one reason or another, were unable to support them.

In the life stories of children immediately prior to the post-war social welfare revolution, the intervention of the state in civil society remained limited. The influence of eugenics and Social Darwinism during this period in relation to thinking about people with learning difficulties was considerable. Yet, the policy impact was less than is sometimes assumed, with far fewer children being assessed as having learning difficulties and placed in separate institutions than was to be the case after implementation of the 1944 Education Act. The eugenics movement had a much bigger impact on general policies of assessment and selection within the ordinary school sector. Children were just as likely to find themselves in institutional care because of the break-up of the family unit following the death, separation or illness of parents as because of any systematic policy on the identification, assessment and treatment of 'defective' populations.

These life stories are particularly interesting because they cover a period of transition during which changing philosophies, ideologies and economic conditions ushered in a major transformation in the identification, care, education and management of people with learning difficulties. The social engineering of the post-war years reconstructed the identities of those whose life stories are told in this chapter. For those who were placed in special education early in their lives, such a placement would frequently put them on to a lifetime path of institutional care. For other participants in this research, learning difficulties was a label that came to be applied to them later in life as a direct outcome of new policy constructions of personal and social responsibilities.

In part, these stories illustrate the subordination of lives under the impact of unfolding social structures of control, but they also illustrate the spaces within which people could negotiate and redefine aspects of their lives. Ironically, these stories also illustrate the mechanisms of control that were beginning to suggest how a new ideology of 'needs' and 'normalisation' was soon going to reformulate in far more efficient ways the policies propounded by the eugenics movement during the early part of the twentieth century.

Alice

Alice didn't remember a great deal about her time in hospital but she does remember that it was a doctor who brought her there. Alice initially attended her local elementary school but, after only a short while, was transferred to a residential hospital for the feeble-minded.

> 'I cried. I didn't want to go.'

After that, Alice never saw her parents again. Now, in her sixties she is still upset and troubled by the fact that her mother died while she was in the home and that she was never allowed to express her grief. She was told of her mother's death by one of her sisters who came to the hospital to break the news. She wasn't able to attend the funeral. Perhaps because she had learning difficulties a decision was taken either that the trauma of attending the funeral would be too great, or that she wouldn't really be able to grasp what was happening. Yet, whatever the reason, and whoever made the decision:

> 'I were upset and crying. I couldn't stop crying. It were awful when she died. No one told me to go to the funeral. They never told me to go nowhere. They wouldn't let me go.'

This event, and the confusion and distress that surrounded it, has left its mark on her life, and even today remains unresolved.

Gertrude

Gertrude did not attend school at all. She remembers being at home and her mother teaching her 'to do sewing and knitting but I can't write'.

She lived with her parents for many years and now lives with her sister. Her life is quiet and uneventful.

> 'Sometimes I go to church. My sister takes me. I've got a stick now so I've got to be careful.'

Gertrude's sister is older and in frail health. It is unclear what would happen to Gertrude should her sister become unable to care for her. But this is not something that Gertrude thinks about.

Beryl

Beryl was born into a working-class family before the Second World War in about 1920. She lived with her parents and two older sisters. Although she remembers always having difficulties with her school work she attended an ordinary elementary school until she was 14. More than anything else, Beryl's school life was dominated by frequent illnesses, with the consequence that her school work suffered and, without the support of her teachers, she fell behind.

> 'At school they tried to learn me to write but that's all I could do really and knitting and that. I didn't do a lot because I was off being poorly and that. I used to have these funny migraines and I missed a lot of school. They never used to bother with me much at school. They used not to learn me. They used to just leave me. They used to leave me to try to do things myself, you see, and being ill I couldn't do a lot.'

For Beryl, school was a place to be at, that is when she was well enough to attend, but not a place to learn. Yet, even without academic progress, she was not particularly troublesome to her teachers and therefore she was tolerated and left largely to her own devices.

Around the time that she left school, Beryl's parents both died, one shortly after the other, and she went to live with an older sister. There was never any suggestion that she should work. Her sister was herself a housewife and the gendered nature of respectable working-class life created its own barriers to wider participation in the community and the world of work. In addition, although much better now than it had been when she was a child, Beryl's poor health had left her frail. Yet, 'learning difficulties' was not a label that Beryl had to contend with in her daily life. Her identity was defined by her relationship with her sister and her sister's family.

When Beryl was about 30 years old all this changed. Beryl's sister died and, faced with the prospect of caring for their auntie, probably for the rest of her life, her nephew and niece declared that she could not continue to live in the house. With neither home nor independent means, Beryl suddenly faced destitution and a decision was taken, she knows not by whom, to send her to Whittington Hall,[6] a 'Home for the Feebleminded'. Thus, at the age of 30, Beryl was assessed as being 'feeble-minded' and placed in institutional care. There she remained for the next fourteen years.

> 'The rest of me family didn't want me. I went to Whittington Hall for three weeks 'cos I was poorly and after that they had a meeting at Whittington Hall and me sister's children told them that they didn't want ever to see me any more. They said they'd finished with me now for good. So the people at the Hall became me family.'

A contemporary history of Whittington describes this 'Home for the Feeble-minded' in glowing terms:

> In the early days of the reception of the mentally deficients, both sexes were received, but ultimately it was found advisable to use the Institution for female inmates only. . . . [It has grown] in importance from the days of accommodating fifty women to the present days when there are within its walls four hundred, including a Staff of over thirty. . . . Few Institutions in the Country are better managed and controlled. The Inmates have everything done to make them as comfortable as possible. They have a separate Chapel provided for services, twice every Sunday with a service midweek taken for the lowest grade by the Rector of the Parish. All the inmates are found useful occupations so far as their mental abilities will allow. An Industries School is provided where the girls are taught needlework, raffia work and sewing, &c. There is also a weaving room, where splendid carpets are woven for the Institutions. Handicraft, domesticity, gardening cooking, &c., are also taught.

Another of Beryl's sisters was also in Whittington Hall. She had been there since she was 18 (placed there straight after her parents died). It is likely that her sister suffered from epilepsy, as did Beryl herself, and this, together with the difficulties in providing family support for a girl on the verge of her twenties led to the placement. Beryl recalled that her sister:

> 'had fits and she was sent to Whittington Hall. I took it hard 'cos they wouldn't let me see her. I wanted to go to see her but the hospital wouldn't let me go in when I was 14. I was 18 before I saw her again. When they put me in there it was nice being with me sister again. She had been there a long time before me. She were a bit unruly sometimes. If anybody said owt to her they upset her but she weren't too bad with us.'

In the late 1970s, Whittington Hall closed down and Beryl was moved into a residential home, but this placement separated her once more from her sister who was moved to a home elsewhere in the town.

> 'I used to do a lot for her and now she's always asking for me but I haven't seen her since Whittington Hall closed. We were moved to different places.'

Beryl has no one to take her the ten miles to the residential home in which her sister lives, but from time to time she does hear stories about her sister from staff in her own home who have been in communication with staff where her sister resides.

Beryl's story graphically conveys the stifling control exercised over the weak and powerless. It emphasises the precariousness of 'place' and the ways in which an identity was created, dependency constructed and control enforced through the structures which were there to support and care for the 'feeble-minded'. Yet, it is important not to see Beryl's life, and particularly her confinement, through today's eyes. To do so would be to victimise her even more. She remains outwardly contented with her life. In telling her story she does not present herself as a victim of a faceless and uncaring system. She rather acknowledges the inevitability of her situation and is thankful for the care she does receive. This might be understood in terms of the domination of the system in constructing her identity, but it also suggests through a glimmer of resistance how this identity is contested and reconstructed. One pleasure in life that makes her eyes shine happened when she was about 50 years old.

> 'I started going to basic education classes. When I went to classes I started learning straight away. Now I go to college.'

Ironically, Beryl's failure to learn at school, which later was to provide a rationale for her being institutionalised as 'feeble-minded', was now being contested in her enjoyment and success at basic education classes. As an example of resistance it is hardly 'earth shattering', yet it conveys her sense of self-dignity and refusal to be bound by labels that were arbitrarily applied.

Jim

Like Beryl, Jim's childhood was dominated by the trauma of having a parent who died young, and the subsequent upheaval of being separated from his siblings and living with relatives.

> 'I were living with me mum and me dad but she died when I were three and me dad didn't want me so I went and lived with me aunty. Then me aunty died and I lived with me aunty's daughter. Me sister and me were split up. Me sister went to live with another aunty. It were a bit upsetting for a while but I got used to it after a while.'

Born just before the Second World War (in about 1934), Jim, like many children of his generation who were later to be labelled as 'mentally deficient', attended an ordinary elementary school.

> 'I went to a school near me aunty's. There were plenty of people there. Some were all right and some weren't. I got on with some of them and some I didn't know. I got into trouble sometimes but I got on with me teachers. I learnt me numbers but me reading and writing weren't very good.'

Yet it was poverty that was the defining condition in Jim's life, not 'learning difficulties'. Life for many working-class families in the inter-war years was dominated by hardship and suffering. For some, the introduction of compulsory secondary education, far from providing an access to opportunity, was an additional burden to be endured. Jim reached secondary school age just when it became compulsory to attend, but the hidden costs of free schooling for his adoptive family were more than they could manage, and therefore:

> 'After a while I had to leave that school and I went to the "ragged school".'[7]

The Ragged School Union had first been established in 1844. They were charitable schools dedicated to the free education of destitute children. Although the number of Ragged Schools had declined (from a high point of 192 schools with an average attendance of 20,000 pupils) as a consequence of the 1870 Elementary Education Act, some, like the one Jim attended, continued to provide education for destitute and orphaned children, supported by charitable subscription.

When Jim went to the Ragged School:

> 'First of all I couldn't tie me own shoe laces. They learnt me to tie me shoe laces. I couldn't tell time either. They learnt you to tell the time and I can tell time now. There were about ten in me class, it was small. They helped with reading and writing sometimes but not often.'

Bernard

Bernard was born in 1924 and went to a Catholic school in a country area.

> 'It was a very small school. You only had two classes. We used to go to school and take a packed lunch every day. We used to walk to school barefoot in summer. It were a Catholic school. Two nuns ran the school. They would come in with your roll book and they called your name out. I never used to have any lessons because I'm not good at me schoolwork. I can't read. Nobody tried to teach me so I did other things.
>
> ''Cos I couldn't do lessons I used to go up to the well for a bucket of water and I put all the chairs round if they were having a singing class. The teacher wanted me to practise thatching so I'd be in a corner of the classroom and I'd go up a ladder with a load of rushes on me back pretending to thatch the roof. Everybody else was doing reading and writing. There were five of us who couldn't read and write and the teacher would have us all doing thatching.

> 'I enjoyed every bit of school apart from the end. I was always being late or early for school because no one told me the time at home. I'd been missing school too and the teacher said if I didn't come to school I'd be taken off me parents. Me granny got the pen and paper out and she says to me mother: 'how old is laddo?' 'I don't really know she says.' So me granny worked it out. 'Do you know how old he is?' she says. 'He's 21.' So they decided that I didn't have to bother with school. So I helped on the farm from then on but I was upset because nobody told me I wouldn't be going back to school.'

Constructing and resisting identities

The life histories described in this chapter illustrate the rational ordering of social life together with the growing role of the state in regulating the lives of its citizens. For example, Alice was hospitalised from an early age and experienced quite profound physical and social segregation. She was quite literally society's outcast, receiving little more than basic care and dehumanised, without recourse to the protection of human rights and without access to human compassion. Her early life was structured within the twin principles of the eugenics movement: first, the isolation of those deemed to be 'defective' from the broader society, thus minimising opportunities for contamination; and, second, the structuring and control of the lives of the 'defective', thus preventing them from entering into the sorts of normal human relationships enjoyed by those living outside of 'disciplinary enclosures'.[8]

Gertrude faced a different form of exclusion, namely exclusion from the wider society through her isolation within the family. The family served as a protective mechanism, ensuring that she was not institutionalised within a hospital, but ironically, and perhaps inevitably, she was institutionalised within the family.

Bernard attended the ordinary school but was excluded from the ordinary curriculum. The curriculum that he experienced was one, put together in a fairly *ad hoc* manner, which marked out his difference from 'normal' children in the school and which could hardly be understood as concerned with social integration, despite its parody of his future working life as a farm labourer. Jim also attended the ordinary school, but his experience of exclusion arose not specifically because of any understanding of his needs and identity in terms of learning difficulties, but rather directly as a result of his poverty.

Beryl experienced exclusion in yet another way. Hers was characterised by her childhood illness, possibly epilepsy, and prolonged periods of hospital treatment that kept her away from school. In other words, although formally attending the mainstream school, she was excluded because of her inability to participate, with the result that she was constructed as incompetent. Later, this was to be formalised when the breakdown of her family situation led to her placement in an institution for the 'feeble-minded'.

In each of the lives described in this chapter, the family and family relationships play a central part in the process of both inclusion and exclusion. Yet, significantly, the formalisation of the label of 'learning difficulties' is less important both in the decision-making process and in the wider representation of the identity of these people than is the relationship of the state to the family. In these life stories we see evidence of the way in which statehood is being constructed through its intervention in the management of family life, through its construction of identities that were deemed to be 'abnormal'.

With Alice this is fairly straightforward in that as an orphan the state took immediate steps to substitute itself for the family. For others, this relationship was less clearly defined and subject to a greater degree of contestation. The experiences of Gertrude and Beryl, for instance, illustrate different aspects of this contestation for control between the family and the state. In both cases, the family initially provided protection from institutional segregation, but for Beryl this was overturned when, at 30 years of age, she was identified as having 'learning difficulties', which provided the rationale for the state's intervention in dealing with her family breakdown.

Conclusion

These five stories describe quite different experiences. The label of learning difficulties was used in different ways and to different effect. They illustrate very well the fact that provisions for the care and management of people with learning difficulties in the first half of the twentieth century were not well developed. Institutional responses were inconsistent and often non-existent. The great 'discovery' of learning difficulties was yet to happen, despite the fact that concerns about a hidden population of feeble-minded children had been mounting throughout the twentieth century. The Wood Report called for the extension of provision to meet what was seen as a growing need. The report lamented the 'unscientific' and unsystematic procedures for identifying what were believed to be large numbers of children with learning difficulties, both outside the school system altogether and within the mainstream schools, whose needs were not being addressed. These concerns, which would eventually be addressed following the 1944 Education Act, were principally focused upon the role of the education system as a mechanism for efficiently regulating social order. They were concerns that paralleled those of the mainstream sector itself. There, regulation relied upon the differentiation of aptitudes and the use of education in determining and legitimating social roles. The role of special education was at one and the same time more straightforward and more complex. On the one hand, special education was concerned simply with the management of those at the margins of society; on the other hand, it was concerned with controlling a threat to the order of society itself. This threat was not so much to be found in the behaviour of those on society's margins as in the implications of an unregulated population for the cohesiveness of a society based upon highly differentiated social relationships, values and power. The exclusion represented in each of these life stories, however, is also illustrative of the boundaries of the exclusive society, and indeed of the dominance of social inclusion as a characteristic of what have been called 'modernist' societies.

Chapter 4

Lives in special education

The post-war expansion

Introduction

The lives of children were dramatically affected by the 1944 Education Act. It shaped the educational system of England and Wales for the next forty years and its impact extended into all areas of education. The Act itself says nothing about special education, other than establishing the Minister of Education's authority to introduce statutory regulations for its organisation and management. However, this legislation was enormously significant in establishing, as it did, the fundamental proposition that (almost) all children were educable at the secondary school level, but that their needs and aptitudes were different. The introduction of universal secondary education meant that the expansion of the school system continued at a rapid pace.

Following the 1944 Education Act, provision for children with special needs also expanded dramatically. Institutions which had previously focused solely upon the medical care of inmates underwent significant changes as their remit became more explicitly educational. Moreover, for the first time large numbers of children were brought into the education system through an expansion of day special schools as well as residential schools.

The structure of the new secondary school system, based on selection by ability, created the conditions under which those new professions that claimed expertise in such techniques could flourish.[1] These techniques, which in any case had originated out of efforts to identify 'feeble-minded' children, were applied widely in the construction of a special school system that would ease what were perceived to be the pressures on the ordinary school system.

This chapter looks at the impact of the expanding system of special education in the post-1944 period on the life histories of three people: Rachel, Keith and Trevor.

Rachel

Rachel was born in 1947 and became part of that early group of children whose education was directly affected by the policy decision to expand special educational provision in the United Kingdom. Her early experiences of special education, however, differed little from those of children caught up in the pre-war special education system. A crucial issue for her, as for them, was the breakdown of family life, when she was separated from her older brothers and sisters and sent to live in a Children's Home.

> 'My mum couldn't look after us. I went to live in a home; in a Children's Home. My mum couldn't look after us. My mum had six kids, three boys and three girls. I'm the youngest.'

An early memory of living in the Children's Home was of having to write home to her family every day. Yet when she was 5 years old, and therefore ready to start school, she was moved from the Children's Home to a residential school. She cannot remember why, and may never have been told, but this placement would have been made under the new 'ascertainment procedures'. These were required under the Handicapped Pupils Regulations that governed assessment and placement in special education.[2] It is not unlikely that a residential school placement was influenced as much, if not more, by perceptions of Rachel's care needs, as against her learning needs. Ironically Rachel's only experience of mainstream school came about when she was temporarily transferred to one because of painting work being done in her residential school. 'If I had paint on my chest it would make me bad', and therefore her special needs necessitated a mainstream school placement!

When she was 11 years old Rachel was moved again, because her residential school only catered for primary aged children. Rachel's new school was a day special school for children who were 'moderately educationally subnormal'.

> 'It was like a boarding school. We had to stop there all day until it was time to go home.'

'Home' was once again a Children's Home. She remembered life in the Children's Home as being happy, but by contrast remembered little about her school experiences. What did stand out in her memory was not school work and learning activities but the humiliation she experienced as a young girl in this environment. One particular incident she recalled illustrated this:

> 'I did P.E. and had to wear shorts with plimsolls. Once I went to P.E. and my shorts were splitting! That was embarrassing. The lads started playing about with me; tormenting me. I was only very young. Not very old at all.'

An incident like this could of course have happened in any school and is not distinctive of special schools. Yet, what it does draw attention to is one of the pervading problems affecting the development of special schools. The post-war expansion of the special school system came about only in part because of concerns about children whose educational needs were not being met in the mainstream sector. Often of greater significance were the concerns of teachers who were suddenly faced with what were perceived to be 'troublesome' children in the newly established secondary school sector.

Boys were much more likely to be labelled as troublesome than girls and therefore more likely to be removed from the mainstream sector and placed in special education.[3] This created particular difficulties in respect of the placement of girls. Girls were generally in a small minority in institutions dominated by troublesome boys. In practice, the distinction between 'maladjustment' and 'educational subnormality' was often tenuous. Therefore, 'troublesome' girls like Rachel, whose needs were the product of social rather than educational circumstances, were more likely to be assessed as 'educationally subnormal' than 'maladjusted' simply because the gender distribution in the former schools tended to be more balanced. This did not necessarily protect girls from bullying, as Rachel's story indicates. What it does illustrate, however, is the role of the special education system in constructing and perpetuating gender stereotypes and gender discrimination.

The next stage in Rachel's education was once again determined not by her educational needs but by another change of Home. As she approached adulthood she was being prepared for adult life outside of residential care and thus was placed in a halfway hostel, receiving educational provision through a day special school.

The constant disruptions that Rachel had experienced in her education, brought about by attempts to meet what were perceived to be her 'social' needs in the absence of family support, were now added to by a period of illness:

> 'I was very ill when I was there [at the day special school] and went into hospital and spent a lot of time in hospital.'

On finally leaving school, Rachel moved to yet another hostel and spent a short time attending a day care centre for people with 'learning difficulties'.

Rachel's entire experience of schooling had been determined by the perceptions of professionals regarding her 'care'. Educational placements had been found for her that fitted in with her residential situation. Sometimes these were residential school placements and sometimes day school placements. From Rachel's point of view, one consequence of this constant disruption was that she had not been able to benefit properly from the education she had received. More than that, it had actually been a significant factor contributing to the 'learning difficulties' that she experienced.

Leaving school and public care after years on the margins of society, Rachel now found herself as an adult without any of the rights and freedoms that adulthood might be expected to bring. Her identity was firmly cast within the framework of 'learning difficulties'. The welfare and education decisions made by professionals about Rachel in those years constructed the context of subordination around which her subsequent struggles as an adult for social status and personal dignity would be fought.

Within a short time of attending the day care centre, Rachel decided that she wanted to find some meaningful work, and after making some enquiries herself she found a job with Remploy.[4]

> 'I went to Remploy and I was there for twenty years. We made corsets, belts, them plastic collars and elastic for bad hands, crutches and walking sticks, and special shoes. I got the job there myself. 'I went there Monday to Friday all day. Sometimes there was overtime on Saturdays but I didn't work overtime. They asked me to but I said "no, I want to go home".'

Despite the fact that Remploy was a firm employing disabled people, holding down a 'proper job' which paid her wages and allowed her to establish friendship networks independent of the 'centre' gave Rachel control over her own life to an extent that she had never previously experienced. Yet, the fact that she could also say 'no' to working overtime, and through this establish her right to spend time in the personal space of her own home, illustrated in a very small but significant way a form of resistance to the controls implicitly imposed by the label of 'learning difficulties'. The job and her ability to resist its demands, as well as to express her freedom through it, created the space in her life through which she could contest the total control and subordination of her childhood years in 'care' and special education.

Eventually, Rachel decided that she had had enough of working in the factory.

> 'In the end I left. I was so fed up with it. I wanted a different job to machining but they couldn't find me another job. That's what I left for. Now I go to a day care centre, Monday to Friday. I do reading and writing there and on Thursday I go to pottery.'

Returning to the day care centre of her own choice after twenty years reinforced her personal control over decisions in her life. It also allowed her to explore new forms of self-development. Yet the context within which Rachel's resistance occurs should not be underestimated. The powerful structures of subordination that it illustrates include her entrapment within services and provision that have been constructed to incorporate a section of the community under the label of 'learning difficulties'. Rachel's life story speaks both of exclusion and segregation, on the one hand, and on the other hand, of the reconstruction of her life within the parameters of what defines the 'normality' of the social order itself. It states the terms of her inclusion and thereby defines the limits of her participation. Her resistance is 'powerful' in the sense of self-empowering but the limits of this resistance also specify the dominance of social structures in her life. She defines herself within those structures. Her resistance both challenges and reconfirms their dominance.

Keith

Keith began his education at his local primary school when he was 5 years old. Within one year he had been transferred into the rapidly expanding special school system. The year was 1959 and the expansion of special education was building momentum.[5]

Reflecting back on his early experiences of special education, Keith was unhappy about the placement and unconvinced of its benefits.

> 'It were a bit distressing being sent to one of them schools because I think if I'd got support [in mainstream school] I wouldn't have had to leave. It were just slowness with the education and stuff that I were having. The learning part, it were a bit hard; you know, reading and writing. Support [in mainstream school] would have been more important.'

The labelling and social segregation brought about by the placement were felt particularly strongly.

> 'My brothers and sisters all went to the ordinary school. I had to have a special bus and it didn't feel nice.'

Its effects on family life were to be long-lasting, but, unlike many of those placed in special education before 1944, for Keith disrupted family life was an outcome rather than a cause of the decisions made about his education.

Keith's criticisms are directed principally at the system of segregation rather than at the nature of the institution.

> 'I don't have sad memories of [special school]. The children and staff at . . . were very good. We'd help one another. I made good friends.'

Yet, the quality of education that Keith received was not of a particularly high standard and did not, in his view, justify the decision to place him in a special school.

'School taught me to write but I didn't learn a lot at school. The teachers didn't have a lot of time really. The annual holidays were too long. I think you get too many. You should only have one every so often. The teachers wouldn't have enough time to support people and they didn't have enough time to see how much support you wanted.'

Special schooling at that time was characterised by the absence of coherent curriculum development. Teachers in special schools very often taught what they wanted, unfettered by national prescriptions and concerns about integrating their curriculum with that of local mainstream schools.

'You got further and further back with your education. I didn't feel I was comfortable with that. We didn't get support workers. It was all the class you know. We had to get together. You had to get on with it.'

In these circumstances, following placement in a special school, reintegration into the mainstream school was unlikely to occur.

The purpose of schooling was hard for Keith to understand. If there was no rationale in terms of the academic curriculum, then should its rationale have focused upon preparation for adult society and the learning of life skills? This latter rationale was not one that accorded with Keith's perceptions.

'School didn't prepare you for being on your own. And we didn't even have any sex education. Nothing about family planning and things like that. When I had a relationship it became problematic so I had to get to knowledge from other people about family planning and stuff like that. School should have given you that information. I didn't even learn anything about washing clothes or cooking.'

Overall, the experience of special education, for Keith, was stifling.

'You didn't get any choice at school. It used to be all about what the teacher wanted to do, whereas it ought to have been a choice what we did.'

The consequences of special schooling, however, stayed with him after he had left school and was trying to enter the world of work.

'I left school when I were 16 and I was unemployed for a while. I was living at home with my parents. I went down to the Job Centre and tried to get a job but I couldn't get one because I was labelled 'Green Card' disabled. It labels you all the time. I got a label having been to

> a special school. I didn't get my first job proper until I was 23. I just did my parents' allotment.'

The 'green card' system, which was designed to support disabled people in obtaining work by requiring large employers to recruit a proportion of disabled people to their staff, in Keith's view actually worked against people with 'learning difficulties'. It was no more than an extension of the labelling he received at the special school. Moreover, it reinforced his sense of difference from his siblings.

> 'I was prepared to do owt for money. My brothers and sisters were all in work.'

When he did find work, it was short-lived, although it did suggest the importance of the comradeship that could be had from working together with others.

> 'I got my first job in the factory when my parents were alive, when I was 19. I were a knife grinder but I was only there for a month. I had to leave because they said it was only a month's trial and I weren't any good at that job. It was all right, the people would get on with you, you know; we would all get on together.'

After leaving school Keith had sought to improve his opportunities for gaining work by attending, first, courses at his local college and, later, Adult Basic Education classes. Attendance at these classes has made a considerable impact on Keith, lasting throughout his life. They not only provided him with skills that he did not have but they also gave him a degree of control over his learning and generally over decision-making in his life that he had not previously had. In this sense his participation in Adult Basic Education was an example of both self-empowerment and resistance to the identity that the school system had placed on him.

> 'After I left school I went to do courses at the College. Then I went to the Adult Basic Education classes. I was doing them for quite a few years until I stopped last year. I went to the Adult Basic Education classes after I saw a leaflet. It were me own choice. I wanted to do them because I could hardly read at first. I've come on with them classes.'

Eventually, Keith did obtain a 'proper job' with the help of his brother.

> 'My first proper job was as a glass collector. I'd seen it in the Job Centre but I couldn't get an interview at first so my brother had a word with his

gaffer and asked if I could get an interview. I did. I went round for an interview on the Friday and got the job from there.'

As it did for Rachel, obtaining paid employment provided Keith with the opportunity to create a space within which to live his life.

> 'I think things were beginning to come together with learning difficulties. Things were changing in the process of the years. You could do different things. My employer looked at me as somebody who had learning difficulties, but someone who was already working there had a daughter who had learning difficulties so they were sympathetic.'

Keith's success in gaining employment also reflected, as he himself observes here, that attitudes were changing towards people with 'learning difficulties'. Of course there remained many people who were attending special schools who were not able to find employment, as well as those assessed as having 'severe educational subnormality' who, prior to 1970, were excluded from any sort of educational provision.[6] However, the expanded special education system was labelling many more people than ever before, capturing within its net for the first time what the Wood Committee had estimated to be that substantial group of less severe feeble-minded children. Thus, the growth of special education created its own tensions. It might appear that people with 'learning difficulties' were finding it easier to find work and move into mainstream society during these years of full employment than had previously been the case. Yet, the simple fact that so many more people were receiving this label in the first place operated as a powerful stigma inhibiting participation in society. In this sense, the new policies of special education had important continuities with the eugenics of the pre-war era. In refining the system of selection through psychological and educational assessments, it had not only become possible to isolate those with 'learning difficulties' for education within a special sector, but it also meant that a more 'efficient' system had been constructed to assist potential employers in matching people to jobs. The special school system had put in place a technology for distinguishing between what in the past had been called the 'high grade mental defective' and the 'low grade'. It had created conditions whereby society and its distribution of opportunities and rewards could be more rationally organised.

Keith's job was in a local workingmen's club.

> 'I went round collecting glasses and enjoying the company. It was like that until 1987 when I got married.'

Getting married confronted Keith and his wife-to-be with a whole new set of social taboos.

> 'I met my wife because she had a flat near me. Her family weren't happy about us getting married. They were very nasty about it. They were a bit frightened of it at first. They didn't think it were right. They didn't think she ought to have a choice on her own. They thought she ought to be treated like a kid.'

Marriage led to new responsibilities and a desire to work more sociable hours to protect his family time.

> 'It were the unsociable hours bit that came in. I think that if I'd stayed working there it would have destroyed me marriage so that's when I left and went back to factory work.'

Keith had little trouble finding work with more sociable hours and soon he had a job sweeping up in a wood-turning factory.

> 'I worked at the factory for thirteen months before I got made redundant 'cause the factory weren't doing very good. I got on with me job all right, cleaning up wood shavings.'

Redundancy was a demoralising blow for Keith, as it was for many people in working-class communities at the sharp end of the de-industrialisation policies of the 1980s. Moreover, for Keith, his acceptance by his workmates as 'one of them' represented his resistance to the label of 'learning difficulties' that had been placed on him as a child. The culture of working life, rather than simply the job itself, was a central feature of Keith's identity.

> 'I was sad about leaving because when I got the job they looked at you as a person.'

The point here is not that participation in the workforce is necessary for people with 'learning difficulties' to find an identity outside this label. Not all people with 'learning difficulties' would be comfortable in the environment of the workplace. The point that is highlighted is that the growing involvement of the state in specifying 'deviant' populations during this period made participation in the culture of their own communities more difficult. It turned social practices that many people would take for granted into serious forms of resistance. The paradox Keith's story reveals is that while the expansion of special schooling was seen by policy makers as offering educational opportunities to many more people with 'learning difficulties', the consequence was that larger sections of the community faced the challenge in adulthood of gaining acceptance within their own communities.

After being made redundant, Keith went back and asked if he could have his old job back collecting glasses at the club.

> 'The hours were still unsociable but it's what I had to do.'

The effect of this return to bar work, as Keith had originally feared, was the disruption of family life. His wife felt isolated, unsupported and neglected.

> 'It was a good time when we were married but the last year of the marriage were bad and we split up and got the divorce bit. The unsociable hours at the club made it hard.'

There were two key points in Keith's life when professional interventions impacted upon him. The first was the initial assessment, when he was a child, that he was 'educationally subnormal' and would therefore receive his education in a special school. The second occurred at the time of his divorce.

> 'After we split up I got made homeless and I went down to the Council on my own and got a Council flat. I wanted to live near where I were before we were married but the Council thought it were a very, very bad idea because my wife was up there. But she had already given her notice and was moving somewhere else so I couldn't see any harm. The place I ended up at isn't very good. Kids out on the street drinking, boozing, lots of drug addicts up there. And the people up there discriminate against people with learning difficulties. They torment them a lot. I get hassle and things like that.'

Now at 42 years of age he was once again confronted with the presumptions of professionals that they were in the best position to make decisions about his life. Keith had been re-housed in an area in which he felt particularly vulnerable to the prejudices and abuse of people who didn't know him. Moreover, the arbitrariness of professional decision-making took no account of the fact that he would be moved away from a community in which he had lived all his life. At this crucial moment the label of 'learning difficulties' embodied the subordination against which throughout his entire life he had struggled to resist.

Trevor

Trevor attended a special school in the 1960s.

> 'I have some happy memories, yeah, happy memories. The teachers were very nice. Sometimes you got told off. If you had been naughty

the teacher told you off but other times it was good. We used to do a Christmas play every year. One year one person, Buffalo Bill I think it was, was ill so they asked me to do it and I did it. Another thing I remember is we used to wash cars. I can remember getting the teacher's car. We could move it out of the garage every morning and put it back every night. Teachers used to steer the wheel and I would push the car. We always washed cars. We washed the teachers' cars and minibuses. We used to check the petrol and oil for the minibus and see if it had got any water. One year, the day of my birthday the teacher and the headmaster came down to get me. Everybody sang happy birthday to me.'

The detail in which Trevor remembers a happy and carefree time at school contrasts with the dull emptiness of the more formal side of his schooling.

> 'I know we did reading and writing and stuff but I can't remember the lessons.'

Moreover, the happy memories of his time at school mask another side of Trevor's experience of special school.

> 'I feel angry about going to a special school. I get angry in my head about why I'm like that. I don't know why I feel angry, I mean I'm always happy.'

Not only is this anger directed at the experience of special schooling but it is directed also at himself for being 'like that'. It is an internalisation of the label that he does not really understand and thus his resistance is, in part, translated into a self-hatred.[7] The very act of resistance reinforces his subordination.

And the consequences of attending a special school persist:

> 'Because I've been to a special school sometimes people out there give people a sort of label. I feel angry about that.'

Since leaving school Trevor has struggled to lead an ordinary life, free of the stigma of 'learning difficulties'.

> 'In my spare time I listen to music, or watch a film on a video, or play my guitar. It's an electric one. I like to go out with my family on trips. My family always lets me choose what I want to do.'

None the less, the label of 'learning difficulties' is a constant part of his life, defining the boundaries of what is possible:

'When I left school nobody talked to me about jobs or anything. I wanted to work in a garage or to take photographs or be famous or something, but no one asked me. The only thing they talked about was things like Centres. You know, telling me that I would have to go to a Centre for people with learning difficulties.'

In the end he had 'no choice':

'I can't remember who picked the Centre for me. I was nervous about going and a bit upset. I were frightened in a way.'

At the Centre Trevor was given work packing 'lucky bags'. The contradictions of this experience mirrored his experiences of school. It gave him a sense of belonging, of companionship and of purpose, and yet it was also experienced as exploitative and ultimately as reinforcing his powerlessness.

'I used to be at the Centre every day packing lucky bags. The work was alright but you'd only get about £4. But now I get nothing at all. The work's stopped. I feel angry about it but there's nothing I can do about it.'

Yet Trevor did eventually seek out alternative ways of expressing his resistance to the label of 'learning difficulties' and its effect on his life, leading to a politicisation of his struggle.

'I belong to a self-advocacy group. That is what the group is about. We've got to take that label off us.'

Despite the constraints that he feels others have tried to impose upon his life, Trevor is imbued with a sense of himself that rises above these constraints. His early desire to be 'famous', to be someone and not to succumb to the labels and limitations that others place on him still comes over in conversations with him.

'If the band takes off I'd like to go touring. We've been to London about three times. And we get paid for doing all the gigs and I put the money in the bank.'

Conclusion

The expanding system of special education after 1944 inevitably led to greater numbers of children being labelled as 'handicapped' and in particular as being 'educationally subnormal'. Despite this there was little clarity about the aims and objectives of special education provision. Cynics might argue that the main purpose served by special schools was the removal of troublesome children from ordinary school, and that with the introduction of universal compulsory secondary education, ordinary schools would have been unable to function at all without this safety net. Yet, the expansion was also informed by the principle that (nearly) all children were educable, and the philosophy was heavily influenced by post-war egalitarian thinking about rehabilitation of those marginalised by the inequities of the past within the core values of a welfare society.[8] Despite this, 'needs' continued to be defined, not in terms of education, but in terms of 'handicaps' identified by medical, or (as in the case of psychometric assessment) pseudo-medical, assessment. The development of a curriculum for children with 'learning difficulties' was haphazard and generally poorly integrated with that within the local mainstream schools. Post-16 opportunities and support with the transition to adulthood were limited and in many areas non-existent. Special education could still be seen as the solution to a wider range of social problems, with placement being defined more by the availability of provision than by catering for different needs.[9]

The life stories related in this chapter all demonstrate evidence of subordination. This does not necessarily mean that their experiences of special schooling were unhappy. Trevor, in particular, tells a story of his schooling that is filled with fond and happy memories. However, the impact of the label of 'learning difficulties' bestowed through special education created the possibility of total control being exerted over them at key periods in their lives. Rachel's life was structured within the kind of provision available to people with 'learning difficulties': special school; Remploy; day care centre. Her resistance took place within those different forms of provision and not in freeing herself from them. Keith who found work that gave him an identity within his own working-class community beyond the label of 'learning difficulties' was none the less disempowered by that label at the critical time of becoming homeless after the break-up of his marriage. Trevor who was never happy with the label and has resisted it throughout his life remained confused by the self-loathing that his resistance to it induced. In each of these stories it is clear that special schooling was not a disaster. Resistance to the label of 'learning difficulties' and its consequences in later life was central to their sense of dignity as human beings. Yet each life story provides insights into the cracks that existed in the policies of rehabilitation and normalisation that dominated the post-war beliefs in social engineering and social welfare.

Chapter 5

Lives in special education

The management of learning difficulties

Introduction

The 1981 Education Act abolished the categories of handicap that up to that time had been used to link educational provision and resources to needs. These categories were replaced by a generic concept of 'special educational needs'. Section 1(1) of the 1981 Act refers to a child having special educational needs 'if he has a learning difficulty which calls for special educational provision to be made for him'. This will be the case where he or she:

> has a significantly greater difficulty in learning than the majority of children of his age; [or] he has a disability which either prevents or hinders him from making use of educational facilities of a kind generally provided in schools.

The significance of this definition was twofold: first, it maintained that 'learning difficulties' exist on a continuum rather than comprising a discrete category of handicap; second, it led to the presumption in assessment decisions that special educational needs are, in part at least, the consequence of inappropriate educational facilities. The predominance of educational thinking about special needs was for the first time established under the legislation.

Yet, recognition of the generic character of special educational needs ironically opens up a debate not only about the ways in which the inadequacy of provision highlights conditions under which existing needs cannot be met, but also about how needs are generated by the inadequacy of provision. The Act seems to assume that special educational needs may arise where the child does not benefit from what is normally available to all children. A more critical view of the relationship between needs and provision might suggest that the failure of any child to learn reflects upon the quality of teaching and learning taking place. It does so because in every educational context there is a dynamic learning relationship between the facilities and activities of instruction and the child. This latter view suggests that special educational needs only exist in terms of the limitations placed upon the rationale, goals and resources of the education system. It might also suggest that by the 1980s the special educational sector had become a mechanism for the creation of needs rather than a system for rehabilitation.

This chapter presents three life stories from young people who received their education in special schools after 1981. The first of these, Karen, did not have 'learning difficulties' in the pre-1981 sense. She was placed in a special school because of physical disabilities, but her story illustrates how being labelled as having 'special educational needs' was a critical factor disadvantaging her learning, and in effect creating learning difficulties. The special school curriculum was increasingly a cause for concern and in the 1980s it was brought into line with that in the mainstream sector. One consequence of this, however, has been a new focus on the mastery of competencies. Wesley's story of his schooling illustrates this development, but more importantly it also shows the lack of consistency between the notion of learning competencies and the transition of young people from special school into adulthood. Michelle was attending college when interviewed and was particularly concerned with her own transition to the world of work. She was ambitious about gaining employment but her story illustrates the struggle to overcome the label of 'learning difficulties' in the face of professional intrusions into her life, controlling her pathway to adulthood. A theme that will be developed in this chapter is that a post-Warnock reconceptualisation of special education has emphasised the management of economically 'useless' populations rather than the rehabilitation of those with the potential to join the workforce. This in turn reflects wider socio-economic changes in societies moving into a period of late modernity.

Karen

> 'The Council originally wanted me to go to a special school when I was 5 because that was their policy at that time. Anyone, who was disabled, no matter what their disability, went to that school and that was it, end of story. And you stayed there until you left and then you sat at home for the rest of your life. And you weren't expected to achieve anything, you weren't expected to get a job.'

However, Karen's middle-class background came to her aid. This was a time of growing concern about the quality of special education and Karen's parents removed her from the special school and found a place in a local primary school 'where my brother went'.

She remained in the mainstream school throughout her primary education. However, when she was 11 she was once again placed in a special school.

> 'I was going to have an operation and somebody thought that I would need to be in a special school. I would have been in plaster for a couple of years and have physio three times a day. I would have needed to be lifted in and out of my wheelchair and things like that. So it wouldn't have been practical to be in a mainstream school.
>
> 'I was there for eighteen months – I was basically out of education completely. If you couldn't be bothered to do any work you got the non-teaching assistants to do it. We had the biggest class and there were seven of us and there were two teachers and a non-teaching assistant. You had someone collect you and take you to the loo and bring you back. I mean, it wasn't like school, you didn't have to work. It was just playtime for us because we literally played with our games all day. It was worthless. I wasted eighteen months. If I had had that eighteen months in ordinary mainstream education I'd have been a lot better off now. It wasn't so much the school, it was the government and the LEA's attitude. We weren't expected to do the eighties equivalent of the National Curriculum because everyone thinks that if you are disabled physically you are also disabled mentally. And we're not! We were doing things in our class that my Mum now teaches in her reception and nursery class.'

Returning to a mainstream secondary school after her eighteen months in a special school was very difficult. The special school had been unable to meet Karen's educational needs and yet that had been the justification for her placement there in the first place!

> 'I was always ahead of everyone in the primary school but when I went back to mainstream education I'd forgotten simple things like doing times tables and graphs and things. I went into the science block that first week and I was expected to be able to do experiments and things! Well, I didn't know what an experiment was because we weren't allowed to do experiments at the special school. They said it was too dangerous and we weren't clever enough as far as the Education Authority was concerned. So that put me back and I needed an awful lot of help to get back. The people in my class were actually a year younger than me because of all the education that I had missed. I didn't know anything. I didn't know what homework was. I'd completely forgotten what I had learnt in primary school. I mean, it was just appalling. I was doing the Fletcher books, which were like maths and books that you work through in reception class, and I was doing those at age 11.'

Once again, it was Karen's parents who stepped in to get her back into a mainstream school. Difficult as this situation was, it does reveal the growing power of parents, particularly middle-class parents, to challenge local authority decisions.

> 'Even when I went to a mainstream secondary school in a way I was still disadvantaged because the LEA had organised non-teaching assistants for me. I had one who had to escort me everywhere I went, including to the loo. And then I had one for science, and one for PE. I was so disadvantaged by that because I wasn't allowed to go with my classmates. I had to wait around for this woman coming. They treated me like a baby. When I was doing my GCSEs the science lady actually wrote down all the answers for me.'

Integration in the mainstream, though a policy objective of the post-Warnock era, was often in practice little more than tokenism. Protected resources would be made available under the statement of special educational needs but these were focused upon direct learning support in the classroom, such as classroom assistants. The larger questions of buildings access, 'learning culture' and the teaching of citizenship through inclusive and democratic school practices were rarely addressed.

> 'The mainstream school was a massive school. There are three separate buildings. One lesson was at the other end of the building and I was expected to manage. Once I got to the correct block I had to go up flights of stairs. Although I now use a wheelchair full-time, in those days I had no choice but to walk. I used my wheelchair to get from A to B but I had to put everything in this one bag on my back and I had to climb two flights of stairs. And by the time I got there I was shattered and I could have very easily fallen asleep in those classes. And then by the time I'd woken myself up it was time to go back downstairs again for the next lesson. It was really hard work especially when you are trying to work towards your GCSEs. The education was absolutely fantastic, I couldn't have asked for more in that department and the teachers were really good but, I think, looking back I wish I had gone to a school that had the same level of education but was more wheelchair friendly.
>
> 'It was hard, it was hard. When I used to come downstairs I often found that my wheels had been punctured or someone had poured water on my cushion. I didn't look whether or not there was water on my cushion. It's not the sort of thing you expect to have to check. So when I sat down, of course, it wet my trousers and then they used to go round telling everyone that I'd peed myself which was extremely embarrassing at 16. Yeah, it was really tough.'

The transition to adulthood was no less difficult or traumatic for Karen. Before leaving school she did work experience in a local primary school.

> 'I helped in the classes, I heard kids read and helped with their sums and the teachers loved me for it because I was a much needed help. Unfortunately, some of the parents complained. "We don't want someone like that teaching our kids thank you!" I was heartbroken because I loved it, you know. It was only a minority but they managed to get a big enough petition. The school said, "Well, we've got to please the parents. You know, we really need you but unfortunately . . ." So I felt disgusted because I could have gone on to be a non-teaching assistant, that's what I wanted to do at that time.'

In 1991 Karen left school and continued her studies at the local college.

> 'Their policy is that disabled people can go there and be taught but you are only allowed to do certain courses which are on the ground floor. We were only allowed to go in the canteen at certain times. We had to tell a member of staff if we went to the loo even. We weren't known as disabled students, we were known as "wheelchairs". What annoyed me most of all was that we weren't allowed to be members of the Students' Union. We weren't allowed near the Students' Union office so we couldn't enrol.
>
> 'We got together and appealed to the local LEA and got the Students' Union involved. It was hilarious. We all went into a meeting between the senior members of staff and the Students' Union and we protested and put signs up and got other students involved. *We didn't win. In fact, we nearly got expelled for it.*
>
> 'We went to the local LEA; we went to the press and they couldn't do anything because it was the college rules. I am really cross because one of my friends who is quite a bit more severely disabled than me always wanted to be a travel agent specialising in holidays for disabled and elderly people but she wasn't allowed on the course at college. We were discriminated against. It was just barbaric.'

After a year Karen left college and started to look for work.

> 'My lack of qualifications let me down but I wasn't given any choice in that matter. I would have stayed on at college if they hadn't treated us so badly. I applied for over 2,000 jobs. I didn't get one of them! I once did a typing test in the middle of the High Street with a marching band going past and I was sitting in my wheelchair. This was going for one of those employment agencies. I did this typing test and it was audio typing!

So I had to listen to this tape whilst balancing the tape recorder and the typewriter on my knee whilst typing and with a marching band going past. I didn't get the job because I only managed 35 words a minute and they wanted 40. I mean, I ended up collaring a policeman to hold the typewriter, you know! It was just unbelievable – absolutely unbelievable. Another time I went for a job as a medical secretary, and they said "Sorry you can't go upstairs you are a fire hazard" – another door closed to me. Me a fire hazard! The only time I'm in danger of spontaneously combusting is when I've had a curry!

'One company came back to me after the interview and said "Although you are absolutely perfect for the job we've decided that if we even thought of employing a disabled person it would ruin the image and credibility of the company." It was just before Christmas and someone said "This is horrific, why don't you go to the press?" So we did. It was on the front page and within about a couple of days I had a job.

'That's what able-bodied people are like. Even when I was pregnant I've had people say "Disabled people shouldn't have children, they should be sterilised at birth." The person who said that was actually a care worker. You get used to it after twenty-three years. You really do. But I'll never accept it, no.'

Wesley

Wesley was born in 1972 and at the time of this research lived at home with his mother. Up to the age of 18 he had attended a local day special school for children with learning difficulties.

'I didn't like it there. I didn't like me teachers. I didn't like being teased. One teacher was alright but some weren't. I got in trouble a lot there.'

Wesley had started his education at a local mainstream school but his mother thought he had learning difficulties and argued for him to go to a special school. According to Wesley he went to the special school so that he could 'get help to get a job' and 'help to do your own ironing and washing and cooking and help doing your own things'.

'I could write my name but I needed to copy it sometimes. I did numbers too. They give you numbers on paper then you copy them. I didn't like it. They keep telling you, oh, telling you what to do. I can do easy writing to copy and easy numbers but I'm not very good at hard maths. I don't like reading. I only like reading football programmes and football books. After a bit they got fed up with me and didn't like it.'

At school:

> 'I was always doing the wrong thing – coming back from dinnertime late. They said "go outside in the corridor and do your work". I come out with some bad words and all that.'

Another time:

> 'The teacher bring this video to watch and the teacher said "you're not watching this video" so I couldn't watch the video and I didn't like it and after that I lost my temper and I was just mad with her. I told her to "get lost bitch and fuck off" and all that. She needed some more teachers to help her. She couldn't cope with me like that.'

Sometimes this frustration was caused by name-calling and bullying:

> 'I get really mad like when people call me things like "dumbo". Something inside gets me so mad, gets me really worked up. I tell them to "get away from me". I don't listen to them. I put my fingers in my ears.'

Overall, school was a painful experience:

> 'I did wrong things, messing around too much, walking out of classrooms, running off. The teachers would bring me home and tell me mum about me. I couldn't hand the teachers. Teachers bossing me around.'

By contrast Wesley's 'Record of Achievement' (RoA), which was put together to show the different work that he successfully completed at school, lists various competencies with ticks against them and teachers' initials. For instance on a 'Retailing Module' there are ticks indicating that Wesley could 'Explain chain of distribution', could 'Explain the initials VAT'. If Wesley had once known what 'chain of distribution' and 'VAT' meant it was very clear that he no longer did. Under 'woodworking skills' the RoA showed that Wesley could use a screwdriver and a knife: 'I can use a screwdriver but I cut me finger with the knife.' Under a section on cooking, one of the competencies which Wesley has learned is 'sanitise working surfaces'. Asked whom this record of achievement was for, Wesley said 'It's for myself and me mother'. Yet, there is very clearly dissonance between this assessment profiling, which clinically and meticulously measures Wesley's educational progress, and his actual experience of schooling.

What is significant to Wesley about his own schooling includes being bullied by other children because of his learning difficulties, his conflict with teachers and his dislike of schoolwork, number work in particular, which he found difficult and uninteresting. The real experience of schooling contrasts sharply with the ideological reconstruction of the nature of education as instrumental reason focused on the learning of discrete competencies and basic skills.[1] For this reason, special education must be seen in the wider context not only of the education system but also of the struggle for power in the wider society. The infiltration of instrumental reason into the special school system reflects the unfolding of structural changes in the organisation of society and the enforcing of a new moral and political order. The 'competencies' agenda within special education reflects the revival of 'child deficit' theories in education and the collapse of the post-war compromise of an 'inclusive society' based upon assimilation and rehabilitation.

Michelle

Michelle left school when she was 16 years old in 1995 after attending two special schools, one primary from age 5 and one secondary from age 11.

> 'All that I remember really was going to play school and then them noticing that I was more hyperactive and them noticing that something was wrong and then they sent me to . . . to try and work out what was going wrong and things like that. I don't really know what was going on. All I know is that I was allergic to squashes.'

Michelle was unconvinced by the reasons for her placement in a special school.

> 'I don't really think I should have been at a special school. Sure, I had problems with some reading of hard words and spelling but everyone has those problems in some stage in their lives. Some of those kids in ordinary schools have problems with spelling and things like that.'

Michelle did identify some positive aspects to her schooling.

> 'I found it was quite good because if you were really, really stuck they would give you help and not just turn round to you and say "Oh come on, you know you can do it just get on with it!" And things like that and I found that school was more understanding in a way and things like that! The subjects were quite good. They would go through it with you and explain it but at college they just give you work and say, "This is what you have to do" and then "Get on with it".'

However, her complaint was not to do with the quality of education she received but rather with being labelled as having 'moderate learning difficulties', and with the lack of say she had in decisions made about her by professionals. The consequences of these decisions were acutely felt and distressing. Yet Michelle has a very clear analysis of her position.

> 'Nothing was discussed with me. All that I know is that it feels as though I've had a kind of like stamp trade mark put on me like saying, "Oh, you've got a mental age of a 12-year-old" and things like that. That's all I know. It makes me feel stupid because I know that I can do better and I could have gone to proper, normal school but they don't see it like that. It's the government that does those kind of tests and makes those decisions.'

Her powerlessness in the face of professional decision-making was again apparent at the point of transfer from primary to secondary school. Her views weren't sought and she had no say in the decision that her secondary education should continue in the special school sector.

> 'When I left primary school and went to secondary school it just happened. I mean, it was just like "Bang, whack, hit ya!" It was just as though like you've been here, you are going here and that is the end of it. Still it may be that that's the same with lots of people, I don't know really. I do find that they could like when you first go there, explain what will happen until you're 19 or whatever, even though you might be a bit young, they could explain what will happen in your life.'

The isolation of special education was absolute.

> 'We didn't get to mix with any normal students. We didn't get the chance to try and learn from them and they didn't get the chance to like try and learn from us, if you know what I mean.'

After leaving school Michelle started at college, in the School of Care Assisted Learning.

> 'I'm carrying on with literature, spelling, reading and writing, and maths which I don't feel that I need to carry on with. They just tack you in any old class. They don't bother asking you what you feel you need to improve on. They just decide what's best for you without even bothering to ask what you think is best for you. They just do what they want basically.'

Michelle's placement at the college came after an interview with the Careers Service. She did have some choices: agricultural college; engineering; health and beauty.

> 'I wanted to do a care course but that's not really what I'm doing. We do first aid and we do health and safety I think it is, but that's it, that's all we're doing. The rest of the things we are doing is computers, cooking, maths and English, human biology and European awareness. In September I'm going on a catering course and that lasts for a year and then after that I'm going to do the caring course. It's best that I'm doing catering because then I'd get a paper GNVQ and NVQ but if I do caring it's not on paper [there would be no qualification obtained].'

Although she is attending college Michelle does not have very much contact with other students, nor does she think of herself as a 'student'.

> 'I feel that we are still being treated like school kids and if we were real students we'd be given a choice of what we wanted – you know, what lessons we felt we needed to do and not just be chucked into any lesson. Because I'm in this centre and because we don't get to mix in lessons like the normal students, it makes me feel as though I'm standing out from the rest of the students and they can pick me out as being slow and stupid.'

She feels that her placement in a special school has put her on a lifetime pathway of disadvantage and discrimination.

> 'Well, I just find that sometimes I get really jealous 'cos other people can do proper work, go to mainstream and things like that and I feel like an outcast so – It makes me feel goddamn angry! It makes me feel as though it will affect me for the rest of my life, as though I'll always have that stamp on me.
>
> 'I wouldn't have been at the centre if I hadn't been at a special school. As far as I know there aren't any students in the centre who went to mainstream schools. But I can see their point of view in a way because if you've been in an assisted learning school all your life, they don't seem to think you'd be able to cope with mainstream. But if they gave you a chance in mainstream and you can learn from the mainstream students and you'd probably be able to make it. But they don't give you chance to do that. So having "special needs", whatever that means, has been quite important in influencing what I've ended up doing now.'

The label of 'learning difficulties' has become one that permeates all aspects of life for an ever-larger number of children. The Warnock Report, for instance, extended the coverage of the label to include 18 per cent of children within the mainstream school who it was argued would have special educational needs at some point in their school lives.[2] It not only constructs a person as incompetent within the sphere of schooling but also extends beyond school to the endless treadmill of training courses that people with learning difficulties are processed through, with very few opportunities for real work. It extends also into the construction of personal and social incompetence within the community and even within the family. The most distressing thing for Michelle is the way this label has been internalised by her mother and sister and used in the course of ordinary family reproaches and disagreements to 'put me down'.

> 'Mum knows it makes me feel like I'm a dummy and stupid. She knows that but the thing that makes it worse is that she's always telling me "Don't be silly, don't be stupid" and things like that and that makes it worse actually. I'd like her to explain it to me and say "it doesn't work like this" and "this is how it works" and things like that. I mean, I know it's difficult for her because she hasn't been in that situation. I know it's hard for people that have been to mainstream to accept that but if they just try and put themselves in your shoes or if they just like have a go at it in an Assisted Learning Centre and if the tutors knew that they went to mainstream but treated them as though they had special needs then they would know how it feels.'

Similarly, just the fact that she has been to a special school leads to her being treated differently by her sister, not all the time but at those moments of sibling rivalry and argument when the label exposes her vulnerability and feelings of 'shame'.

> 'My sister and me can be having a perfectly normal conversation and she turns round and says "Don't be so thick, Michelle!" – like that in front of her friends. And that makes me feel so small and it makes it so much worse – that's one example.
>
> 'Most of the time I get on with me sister well but sometimes we do fight like cat and dog. But I find that's below the belt! She's kind of using the fact that I've been to a special school and have special needs or something to have a go at me. She's always done that.'

Revenge can be sweet! But it doesn't take the sadness away.

> 'Apart from giving her white bath salt and pretending it was salt and putting salt in her tea and being bitchy about her there's no other real way that I can get at her because she's 21 now.'

Teachers, too, can be insensitive.

> 'Sometimes if I get really, really stuck and I ask for help sometimes some of the teachers in college say, "Oh come on Michelle you can do it!" and,

> "Oh don't be so silly you can try it and have a go" and talk to you like you were a baby or a toddler still and that really gets to me.'

Opportunities for resistance to this stifling label at college are also limited. Michelle describes one such act, which almost inevitably ends in the reassertion of the teacher's dominance and through this the dominance of the mechanisms of control and order that devalue her ideas and reinforce her place on the margins of 'personhood'.

> 'When we are cooking at college we have to line up to get our ingredients and I'm so used to having the kitchen to myself and cooking on my own – just using a cookery book in front of me. I tried to get the tutor to show us the different ways that she could do it. I said to her: "Why can't we get the ingredients ready first, and then get on with cooking them and have whatever time we've got left at the end to do a writing assessment instead of sitting down and watching the demonstration before we can get cooking?" But she like just fobbed me off saying "Oh no, I've been doing it for years, I find this is the best way" and things like that and it just seems to me as if it's going through one ear and out the other. They don't listen to the student's point of view and their suggestions and that really, really pees me off. But, I'm not going to have anyone running my life and telling me what's best for me. I'm not going to take that, not any more. I'm just going to stand my ground.'

Conclusion

The significance of resistance, as Giroux argues, is its revealing function. It contains within it a critique of domination and provides opportunities for self-reflection and for struggle.[3] The stories told in this chapter illustrate the powerful structures of dominance that have grown up in the late twentieth century to control and manage deviant populations. In particular they illustrate the changing nature of special education in the latter part of the twentieth century. This includes the extension of the label to a greater number of children as well as the extension of provision beyond schooling, thus tying increasing numbers of adults into a regime of perpetual training. Yet this occurred at the very time at which young people with special educational needs were being excluded from the labour market. The special education system experienced tension between the new policy of 'lifelong learning', with its emphasis upon individual responsibility for training, and the problem of 'the costs of educating young people who might not be economically profitable to society and who did not fit into a human capital equation'.[4] Increasingly this dilemma was being reflected in policies focused upon the management of populations who were unemployable in the market conditions of the late twentieth century.

In their different ways, the stories told in this chapter speak to reflection on the structures and processes that enforce subordination, and yet articulate a refusal to be bound within them. The outcomes from these moments of resistance vary. Karen, partly because of her social class background, was able to mount an effective resistance at various points, challenging decisions made about her by schools, college and employers. In this struggle her life story continually revealed points of domination at which attempts were made to control and marginalise her life within society. Wesley's story shows how the difficulties he found in articulating his resistance in ways 'acceptable' to his teachers and other professionals reinforced his subordination. Yet, Wesley's life story also illustrates the gap between the experience of special education and its supposedly post-Warnock, inclusive educational objectives. Located within a much broader context of economic and socio-political realignment, the introduction of a competencies-based curriculum within the special school sector parodies the logic of school reform, revealing a new unwillingness or inability to accommodate difference. Michelle's life story, like Karen's, clearly indicates a strong will to resist the identity imposed upon her and to maintain her dignity in the face of the disabling label of 'learning difficulties'. However, her story reveals the structures through which her life is externally controlled and directed. The extension of special educational provision beyond school leaving age was a key reform introduced by the 1981 Education Act. Michelle's story, however, shows how this extended provision can operate to sustain the separation of people from the mainstream of society at the point of their transition into adulthood. In Michelle's case, college perpetuated her childhood status and as such legitimated her exclusion from the wider society. The intrusion of professional decision-making inhibited the transition to adulthood by denying her the opportunity to locate this transition within the context of her rights as a citizen.

Chapter 6

Special education and the politics of educational reform

Introduction

In this chapter it is argued that the transformation from pre-modern to modern times was characterised by the paradoxical relationship between the individual and society and the 'problem' of social order. Resolution of that problem was sought in a rationalist model of the social world in which a natural order of progress unfolded through the assimilation of difference within a homogeneous society. It is argued that it is within the ideological framework of this dominant rationalist conception of order that the growth of the eugenics movement in the late nineteenth and early twentieth centuries can best be understood. It is further argued that there is continuity between the pre-war eugenics movement and the post-war reforms aimed at social inclusion and the treatment and rehabilitation of those who are different. This continuity lies in part in a social compromise that limited the radical impact of the reform movement but also in the ideology of a rational order based upon a highly differentiated social inclusivity. This hegemony was only seriously challenged with the collapse of the post-war compromise in the 1980s which ushered in a radical break with the past. The fragmentation of order and the decline of civil society not only created the diversity of individualism but also required it. From that point on, social and educational policy were no longer concerned with compensation and assimilation but concerned instead with the policing of moral boundaries and risk management.[1]

Rationalism and the contradictions of modernity

From its early philosophical origins, rationalism provided legitimacy for a new social order. Yet, more importantly, it offered a new way of understanding the world and of representing the place of social agency within it. It provided a vision of what was possible for humankind if it embraced scientific thought, including possibilities for the creation of a social order in which humanity would be free from the constraints of God and nature. It promised a social order centred upon human rather than spiritual values, upon possibility and progress rather than the traditions and certainties of the past, and upon a belief in the rational control of futures rather than acceptance of the arbitrariness of nature or the mysteries of heaven.

Within pre-modern societies difference was a natural part of life, a life in which everything had its place and was destined to stay that way. Yet by the sixteenth century this divine certainty was falling apart in the face of radical social and economic change based upon the production and exchange of value, with capital and labour as two dimensions of a dynamic and unpredictable force of social transformation. Social and cultural diversity exploded from this new social and economic order. The age of modernity had arrived. Yet its consolidation was dependent upon reconciliation of the contradictions of diversity, on the one hand as a driving force for the self-reproduction of modernity through innovation and change, and, on the other hand, as de-stabilising and fragmentary.

The question of how to secure a stable social order within which diversity could flourish as a catalyst for renewal was to become a central concern of modernity. It was in providing this necessary reconciliation that the 'virtue' of rationalism lay. Rationalism offered an understanding of the world as a place in which order resides. The unfolding purpose of life, moreover, was seen not only as being for the benefit of humanity but also as the product of human activity. Rationalism provided modernist society with both the means of its realisation and the mechanism for controlling the unpredictability of the social diversity that threatened to undermine it. Rationality, human rationality, entailed the objective condition of human life as its own product. A rational conception of humanity implied the exclusion of irrationalism from human affairs together with the possibility of rehabilitation, treatment or correction. In pursuit of these dual ends the specification of difference through observation, classification and regulation quickly became the hallmark of modernity.

Zygmunt Bauman[2] has argued that what is distinctively modern is the concern with order and the fear that unless some action is taken order will dissipate into chaos. 'What makes it [chaos] so disorderly is the observers' inability to control the flow of events. . . . In a modern society, only the vigilant management of human affairs seems to stand between order and chaos.'[3]

However, Bauman also argued that this rationalist ideal is not only an impossible ambition to realise but also highlights the contradiction which 'resides in the very project of *rationalization* inherent in modern society'.[4]

> Rationality is a two-edged sword. On the one hand, it helps human individuals to gain more control over their own actions. . . . On the other hand, once applied to the environment of individual actions – to the organization of society at large – rational analysis may . . . achieve an

> exactly opposite effect: constrain individual freedom. So, the possible applications of rationality are intrinsically incompatible and doomed to remain controversial.[5]

Modernist society is constructed upon a foundation stone of the contradictions between society and the individual. Individual creativity, innovation and freedom are the life-blood of the renewal and regeneration upon which modernity is dependent for its existence. Yet, constraint of individual difference within the unanimity of rational homogeneity is paradoxically the mainstay of the social cohesion of the modernist project. This tension is continuous and the source of both subordination and resistance.

Assimilation and the policy contradictions of inclusion

A belief in the rational ordering of the world, and therefore in the possibility of its principles and structures being accessed through rational enquiry and then manipulated by rational action, increasingly informed an interventionist social policy agenda during the nineteenth and twentieth centuries. This policy is characterised, however, not by exclusion but rather by inclusion through the assimilation of difference and diversity. The 'vigilant management of human affairs' focused upon the identification and classification of those human attributes that threatened the rational model of 'man'. Yet, in identifying and classifying these attributes, the aim was not to cast those who held them out of society. Unlike the leper colony of the pre-modern world, and the 'ship of fools'[6] at the beginning of the modern world, the chaos that threatened the rational ordering of things was to be disarmed, treated and assimilated within the realm of reason. The essence of scientific rationalism lay in its claim to understand and predict those differences that ostensibly lay outside its realm. By so doing, interventions could be targeted which would change behaviour and thereby tame the chaos of the unknown. The modernist project relied upon rational science to provide mechanisms not simply for the exclusion of chaos from its world but rather for the incorporation of what appeared chaotic within its own system of thought; that is, the reformulation of chaos as order, and the rehabilitation of the irrationally disordered. It was concerned with giving identity and meaning to that which appeared chaotic, and with providing treatment for those outside the domain of rationality, with the aim of inclusion through rehabilitation into the social order of rational society.

Thus, modernism was based upon an assumption of a society that both defined the parameters of rational behaviour and sought to neutralise or absorb difference through mechanisms of inclusion. Exclusion occurred not as a central defining process of social relationships but operated on the margins of the accepted social order. It was a mechanism for managing chaos that *for the moment* could not be understood and could not be rehabilitated within the prevailing social order. For this reason, exclusion was an extreme measure that forced the rational world to be confronted by the 'chaos without'. Exclusion represented an admission of the failure of the project of modernity and, for that reason, the violence of its response could be extreme. The thrust of the modernist project remained an inclusionary one; it was a project that built upon rational knowledge to manage the identities of its citizens. Social progress was embodied in the successful incorporation of difference within a reality that was fairly homogeneous and therefore unchaotic.

The inclusionary project of modernity focused not upon the acceptance of difference, but rather upon the assimilation of difference. Differences between people obviously existed but they were sanitised and made safe by the structures of a social order that gave them their place in the world, a place that was to be accepted without question. The inclusion or assimilation of difference within the social order was its fundamental mechanism of control. That which lay outside was dangerous and threatening, not because those people excluded from this world were a threat of themselves, but much more because they threatened to undermine the order within. Thus, the inclusionary project of modernity extended across all areas of social life. It formed, for example, a cornerstone of the policy of empire. Similarly, it was central to the introduction and expansion of a system of universal education towards the end of the nineteenth century. The 'chaos' of national and tribal differences was assimilated into the order of empire in just the same way as the working classes (demonised for the 'chaos' and disorder of their lives) were assimilated into socially useful labour by the inclusivity of the factory and the school.

Throughout the twentieth century, education was at the cutting edge of the modernist project of inclusion. The refinement of procedures for testing and measuring children's abilities and performance created possibilities for maximising the effectiveness of schooling as a system for maintaining social control and perpetuating social roles and rewards. Exclusion, when it occurred, operated at a very high threshold – hence the relatively small numbers of children who were identified as 'feeble-minded' and incarcerated in segregated institutions. However, the violence of responses to those on the margins of the social order, both in language and through policies of isolation, segregation and sterilisation, made manifest the fear of chaos that haunted modernity. The management of morally, mentally, and criminally deviant populations was driven by the idea of a differentiated but inclusive humanity which was threatened by the degeneracy of those on the margins.[7]

Post-war reform and its contradictions

The years following the end of the Second World War witnessed wide-ranging social reform. Education was at the centre of the reform movement, as evidenced by a new philosophy of social inclusion embodied in the 1944 Education Act. Education was a key to change in society, both for reformers who saw it as the catalyst and vehicle for realising the aspirations of the masses, and for those at the forefront of the new economic revival who saw it as the means of preparing a skilled and motivated workforce.

It has become fashionable since the late 1970s to denigrate the significance of the 1944 Education Act in providing educational opportunities for children with 'special educational needs' and establishing the principle of inclusion in respect of education. It is criticised for promoting segregated education on a previously unimagined scale and for institutionalising the dominance of a medical model of disability within education, under the control of a professional bureaucracy which used the system to consolidate its own social power. Such criticisms may not be without foundation, particularly in respect of the way these reforms were to be subsequently implemented, once the immediate impetus for reform had dissipated. Yet, it remains the case that the whole programme of post-war social reform, not just in England but throughout Europe and America, was founded upon an acceptance of the principle of social responsibility for disadvantaged individuals and groups.

There is both continuity and difference between the eugenics movement of the late nineteenth and early twentieth centuries and the policies of normalisation that were adopted after 1945. In one respect, the policies of the post-war era represented a radical break with the past. The post-1945 political ideal was centrally concerned with extending both opportunities and citizenship to people who in the past had been marginalised and disadvantaged within their own society. Thus, post-war special education, far from enacting a policy of exclusion through the rapidly expanding special school sector, actually represented an attempt to engineer an inclusive society in which the needs of all citizens were addressed through schools which were designed to meet their needs. Yet, this differentiation of needs reflected the continuity between post-1945 'normalisation' and pre-1945 eugenics. The highly structured, differentiated character of society remained.

The engineering of social reform was fundamentally framed by the nature of regulatory control within modernity: that is, by the assimilation of difference within the boundaries of a homogeneous social order. Society may be highly differentiated but this differentiation is contained by a social structure that is both assimilative and homogenising, and therefore controlling. Each man and woman has a place and knows where that place and its boundaries are. Special education, rather than excluding the child from participation in society, in fact located the child and provided opportunities within society;

yet this process of inclusion did nothing to challenge the nature of this social order as one within which diversity must be assimilated and therefore controlled.

The 'inclusive' character of these reforms is suggested by what McCulloch has described as 'education as a civic project'.[8]

> 1944 could be read as the high-water mark of education as a civic project in this country. Educational reform was seen not only as a means of achieving equality of opportunity, but also as a way to enhance citizenship. This project involved a strong sense of the power of education to foster social solidarity and cohesion.[9]

However, McCulloch goes on to argue that although the reforms of the 1940s pursued a strongly civic goal, they lacked the means to achieve this goal,[10] contradicted as it was by the tripartite divisions of 'academic', 'technical' and 'vocational' education that lay at the heart of the 1944 Act. The special education project of 'education for all' suffered a similar fate.

That the 1944 Education Act was a compromise, and a compromise that diverted the education policy agenda away from a transformatory politics, has been widely argued. Well before the Second World War, Tawney maintained that: 'The English educational system will never be one worthy of a civilized society until the children of all classes in the nation attend the same schools.'[11]

The introduction of compulsory post-elementary education established the principle that (almost)[12] all children are educable and therefore that their educational needs should be met within the school system. This was a profoundly inclusive policy but it also had consequences that encouraged the growth of separate forms of provision for the disabled. This reflected a fundamental contradiction in the philosophy of the Act itself. While the Act introduced the principle of 'education for all', it organised this universal education on the basis of a differential understanding of children's needs. Separate provision for the disabled, therefore, was seen in precisely the same way as was separate 'academic', 'technical' and 'vocational' education. The failure of the tripartite system to challenge the hierarchies of social and economic power and privilege embedded within it was similarly reflected in the criticisms subsequently directed at special education and its system of categories.

The Handicapped Pupils and School Health Regulations of 1945[13] identified eleven categories of handicapped pupil, later amended to ten.[14] Local authorities were empowered to request a formal certificate of 'ascertainment' from a school medical officer where a child was identified as suffering from a condition described by one of the categories of 'disability of mind or body'. Following ascertainment the child would be placed in a special school. Ascertainment was not actually a requirement for special school placement.

Section 34 of the 1944 Education Act was explicit in stating that formal ascertainment was needed only when an LEA wished to impose attendance at a special school against parental wishes. None the less, local authorities very often ascertained all children placed in special schools.

> This served to emphasise the separate nature of special education, with an implicit assumption that 'special' education could only be provided in schools or classes recognised by the DES as efficient for the education of children with a particular category of handicap. The formality helped to ensure that transfer from special schools to the mainstream was a rare event.[15]

In consequence, the 1944 Education Act reinforced the division between ordinary and mainstream schools and in so doing emphasised the stigma of special education.

The post-war expansion of special education

The expansion of special education following the introduction of the 1945 Handicapped Pupils regulations was phenomenal. In 1950, 15,173 children were ascertained as being moderately educationally subnormal. By 1976, this number had risen to 66,838.[16] The rationale for this expansion had largely been humanitarian. The optimism of the post-war period meant that old fears of difference had diminished and there was a desire for openness in society and for greater tolerance of difference. An extended period of prosperity together with the post-war desire for a 'new social order' encouraged diversity and experimentation. It also encouraged rethinking of the old eugenics that had held such important sway over the development of special education before 1944. The new post-war policies were policies of 'inclusion'. Education was to be the vehicle for building a new society based upon the needs of the country's future citizens. The expansion of special education, therefore, was centrally concerned with extending opportunities and with including all groups within society in the new order.

What precisely this new order represented, however, was to remain ill-defined and little was said about transforming the socio-economic relations of power. In the 1960s, in particular, the rhetoric of the 'white heat of technological revolution' and the 'permissive society' swept society forward without too much reflection on the limits of inclusion and on who was defining its character. After all, we had now all become part of the middle class![17] Yet, there remained some unsettling facts about the expansion of special education.

Throughout this period, there was a gender imbalance of approximately three boys to every two girls identified as being ESN(M). In addition, there was a particularly striking ethnic imbalance. In 1972, children of

Caribbean heritage constituted 1.1 per cent of all children in maintained primary and secondary schools but 4.9 per cent of all children in ESN(M) schools.[18] These statistics were suggestive of darker forces that would challenge the dream of an ordered world based upon a rhetoric of the assimilation of difference in a classless society and the end of dissent. Enoch Powell's 'Rivers of Blood' speech[19] might have been widely seen as exaggerating the likely consequences of immigration but it was to be taken as prophetic by some and as a call to action by others. Soon it was to directly inform the immigration and citizenship policies of successive Conservative and Labour governments.[20] The war in Vietnam became the clarion call for opposition to the shallowness of a value system based on aspirations to middle-class comforts built upon the suffering of a dying colonialism. And, arguably, most important of all, traditional class antagonisms resurfaced as the party of reform, the Labour Party, attempted to make working people pay for the collapse of its social experiment with capitalism.[21]

The struggle to sustain educational reform

The tripartite system of education introduced by the 1944 Act, despite reformist ambitions, had ultimately been concerned with engineering a cohesive and inclusionary social system which maintained power in the hands of dominant social interests. The expansion of a fourth stream of separate special education for those who could not manage in, or would not be managed by, the secondary modern sector was similarly concerned with including all sections of the child population, even the most troublesome, within a single differentiated but interrelated system. However, by the 1960s a new surge of reform was challenging the inadequacies of the 1944 Act.

The comprehensive education reforms of the 1960s, often bitterly fought, implicitly challenged the logic of a separate system of special education. The campaign for the integration of children with special educational needs within the mainstream school sector drew directly on the arguments of the proponents of comprehensive schooling to demand inclusion as a human right, together with equal access to educational opportunities for progression. By 1970, comprehensive schools had triumphed. However, 'although they had succeeded in discrediting and supplanting the secondary modern schools', the outcome was one in which the grammar school and the secondary modern school 'were yoked together under a single label, but the resilient traditions of differentiation remained as active as ever'.[22] The struggle for inclusive education still had a long way to go. It was not until the Warnock Committee on 'Special Educational Needs' reported in 1978 that the principle that integration was preferable to segregation entered the rhetoric of educational policy. By that time, the educational agenda had changed quite dramatically and rhetoric was to speak much louder than action.

The Plowden Report, although concerned with primary education, was none the less particularly important in signalling the significance of social and environmental factors for educational achievement, suggesting how schools could compensate for social and economic deprivation through an infusion of resources and a more flexible approach to individual learning needs.[23] The Plowden Report was also significant in that it rejected the idea that educational 'handicap' arises from individual deficits and acknowledged that there should be a collective responsibility towards those individuals who experienced learning difficulties in their education:

> . . . special need calls for special help. . . . We ask for 'positive discrimination' in favour of such schools and the children in them, going well beyond an attempt to equalise resources. Schools in deprived areas should be given priority in many respects. . . . The justification is that the homes and neighbourhoods from which many of their children come provide little support or stimulus for learning. The schools must provide a compensating environment.[24]

This view was to have important consequences for the future thinking about special education in Britain. However, the curriculum reform movement of the 1960s, which was closely associated with the child-centred philosophy of the Plowden Report, largely passed the special school system by. The special school curriculum came in for particular criticism and did little to convince parents and other observers that special schools were providing 'special' education. Teaching was poor, record-keeping inadequate, science ignored, and preparation for life after school often inappropriate.[25]

By the 1970s, there existed a large and costly system of special educational provision outside of the mainstream school sector which largely catered for 'troublesome' children with learning difficulties and behavioural problems. Yet, as Tomlinson's study[26] of the assessment of children identified as 'educationally subnormal' showed, the procedures for categorising educational needs in terms of 'handicap' were often the product of different and competing professional interests. Assessments tended to be based on assumptions that were rarely made explicit by professionals. These were derived from professionals' perceptions of their own roles and interests rather than from any 'objective' assessment of the child's needs. The system of categorisation served in practice to reinforce the 'expertise' of professionals while operating as a bureaucratically convenient, if crude, mechanism for rationalising the redistribution of resources encouraged by the civic project of the 1944 Act.

Special education had assumed a logic of its own in which it simply served the interests of the mainstream sector, by removing troublesome children, and the interests of professional groups, whose 'specialist' identities were legitimated by the continuing existence of the system. It was a logic, however, that was to bring the system into conflict with the broader social and political context in which it was situated. Changes in the social and economic structure of the modern world began to have radical effects upon the established mechanisms for maintaining social order through differentiation and assimilation.

The politics of 'need'

The Warnock Committee, set up in 1974 in response to a growing disenchantment with the 1944 framework, was to have a wide-ranging influence upon the subsequent development of special educational policy and practice. Not all the report's recommendations were translated into legislation, although nearly twenty years after publication of the report its influence can still be seen in the area of special education policy (for instance in the Code of Practice on the assessment of special educational needs).[27]

The recommendations of the Warnock Report included:

1. abolition of categories and their replacement by a generic concept of special educational needs that emphasised educational criteria (not medical);
2. acknowledgement that up to 18 per cent of children experiencing learning difficulties in mainstream schools do so because of special educational needs;
3. multi-professional assessment and parental involvement in the assessment and decision-making processes;
4. extension of special needs assessment procedures and provision to include children of pre-school age;
5. extension of special educational provision to take account of the needs of young adults in further education.

The radicalism of the report was reflected in the fact that for the first time schools were recognised as a context within which children's educational needs might be created. This is significant because it implies that the educational needs of a child may vary according to factors occurring within the school attended.

> In such cases, assessment may need to focus on the institution, the classroom setting or the teacher as well as the individual child and his family if it is to encompass a full consideration of the child's problems and their educational implications. This needs to be borne in mind by all who take part in assessment.[28]

Additionally, the Warnock Report recommended greater coherence being given to special educational policy through a framework of assessment and provision that would address the needs of children from pre-school through to post-16.

At the heart of this system was the professional, and the Warnock Report, despite its much-vaunted chapter on 'Parents as Partners',[29] represented the high point of professional autonomy and dominance in the special education system. Kirp[30] has suggested that the Warnock Report was underpinned by naivety. The report's view of the benevolence of professionals working as experts on behalf of an ever-expanding clientele ignored the professional interests that lay behind this benevolence. Yet the economic context in which this managerial model of 'consensus' was located is highly relevant. Whereas the model may match the demands placed on professionals during periods of economic growth and social reform, it is a model that is subject to increasing tensions during periods of social and economic upheaval and dislocation when resources are scarce and more aggressively fought over.

Historically, the power of professionals in relation to special education is based upon their role in mediating between the state and the individual recipients of their interventions, and has been characterised by authoritarian theories of knowledge that necessitate the reconstruction of 'difference' as 'deficiency'. Professionals become the guardians of and gatekeepers to 'normalacy'. Professionalism provided a technology, a deeply anti-democratic technology perhaps, but one that, despite obvious tensions, reflected a reconceptualisation of social policy in terms of the role of the state as the vehicle for public solidarity.

The Warnock Report does need to be seen within the overall context of an attempt to construct a more rational framework for identifying and dealing with children failing in, or failed by, the mainstream school system. In this respect, the recognition by Warnock that up to 18 per cent of children in the mainstream sector may have special educational needs at one time or another and that these needs can and should be addressed using the resources normally available to those schools is highly significant.

The 'discovery' by the Warnock Committee of 18 per cent of children with 'special educational needs' within the mainstream school is reminiscent of the eugenicist 'discoveries' of the past.[31] We could see this latter 'discovery' as reflecting concern about the academic failure of large numbers of children within the mainstream sector, and therefore as representing a critique of the school system, contributing to the work of early school effectiveness researchers.[32] On the other hand, it is hardly unimportant that this discovery was revealed in the wake of the raising of the school leaving age to 16 and at a time when there was a growing crisis of youth unemployment, accompanied by concerns about delinquency and social disaffection. In the context of an enforced extension of compulsory education for young people who neither wanted it nor benefited from it, together with restricted employment opportunities, the educational label of 'special needs' conveniently legitimated the educational and socio-economic disadvantages experienced by young people.

It embodied an ideology of individual failure (be it failure of the child or of the school) that delegitimated any discussion of 'inclusion' in the context of a wider political critique of the social relations within which education policy is framed and contested. In this respect, the Warnock Report can best be understood in relation to the collapse of the post-war social compromise.

The regulation of failure

Regulation theorists have argued that the institutions of the state are underpinned by modes of regulation which institutionalise conflict and confine it within certain parameters compatible with the maintenance of social order.[33] The intervention of the state in education thus became a central feature of state formation in the late nineteenth and early twentieth centuries. The social compromise of 1945 lay in the preservation of the dominant values of capitalism. It did so through the creation of mechanisms to alleviate the social cost endemic in the incoherence of economic individualism. These mechanisms included the partial regulation of markets through the intervention of the state and the regulation of social disadvantage through the welfare state. Whereas liberal individualism had represented rights as asserted always in defence of private interests, welfare rights were acknowledged as legitimate claims on the state to support those people who were most disadvantaged by capitalist forms of production and distribution. However, the justification for such intervention was not primarily moral. Rather, it lay in attempts to correct and improve upon the market in order to optimise the allocation to choices through the 'Pareto principle', which maintains that improvements in the social condition of one individual which do not make others worse off are ethically neutral.[34] The provision of welfare benefits is, in theory, a form of insurance to which all members of society potentially have access.

Needs theory has had a central place within the welfare rights discourse and has been a significant feature of the development of special education systems across Europe since 1945. There was an assumption that educational needs could be accurately assessed by reference to some assumed minimum or norm that then legitimated the redistribution of 'social' wealth.[35] Significant deviations from the norm would be identified as indicative of 'special' needs requiring the allocation of compensatory resources.[36] Thus, needs theory retained the focus upon the individual that was characteristic of pre-war liberalism while advocating the role of the state as the protector or guardian of citizens against the anarchy of private interests. The role of social democracy was to regulate competing individual interests while providing a cushion of support for those whose needs were marginalised by the social outcomes of this competition. This view of social democracy assumed, however, that the state is neutral. Yet such a representation is deeply problematical.

The society in which we live is one 'where production for profit remains the basic organizing principle of economic life'[37] requiring 'the disciplining of labour power to the purposes of capital accumulation'.[38] This in turn gives rise to contradictions in the regulatory role of the state in social and economic life. The viability of the welfare state lay in the provision of a context that supported the accumulation of capital. However, welfare policies exposed the contradictions between the political role of the state in legitimating the accumulation of capital and the economic consequences for the capitalist system of the appropriation of surplus value by the state.[39]

The Warnock Committee's 'ludicrous'[40] recommendation that 20 per cent of children would have special educational needs at some point in their school lives highlights the contradictions within and between the political and economic domains of capital accumulation. First, the identification of 20 per cent of children with special needs represented a logical extension of post-war policies supporting the inclusion of marginalised children under the protection of the welfare state. It was one of the policies that comprised the post-war social contract between capital and labour, facilitating the continued accumulation of capital. Second, it was the outcome of political agitation for humanitarian reform that was independent of the interests of capital accumulation. In other words it reflected the discontinuities and contradictions between the political interests of capital and the constitution and policies of the state.

Third, as already argued in this chapter, this recommendation legitimated the rising youth unemployment of the 1970s resulting from economic downturn and the crisis of capital accumulation. It presented a policy solution to growing concerns about how the consequences of economic crisis were being reflected in delinquency and social disaffection among young people. Fourth, it turned attention towards mainstream schools and the inadequacies of curricula and pedagogic practices, proposing an alternative special educational discourse based upon school reform and inclusion within the mainstream school. In advocating a policy of inclusion the Warnock Committee, whether intentionally or not, was responding to the rapidly changing political and economic agendas of the late 1970s, famously initiated by James Callaghan's Ruskin College speech,[41] which demanded new systems of flexibility, accountability and, most of all, cost-effectiveness from educational services. The reining in of the state by capital had begun!

The 1981 and 1993 Education Acts

The 1981 Education Act took up many of the recommendations of the Warnock Report, establishing a new framework for managing special education assessment and decision-making. In particular, categories of 'handicap' were abolished and replaced by a generic concept of 'special educational needs'. 'Special needs' were assumed to be educational and not medical and to exist on a variable continuum.

The significance of this was twofold. First, the assumption of a necessary link between 'impairment' and educational need was rejected. Needs would be identifiable by an assessment of learning needs in context. Thus, the resources available within a particular school, the curriculum and its delivery, and the skill of teachers, as well as factors in the wider community impacting upon opportunities and achievement, were all relevant factors. Second, these needs might vary both across different contexts and across time. The identification of 'special educational needs' was not to lead to a life-long labelling but rather to a flexible procedure for managing intervention and resources. This was reinforced by the introduction of procedures for annual review of statements of special educational needs. This framework was subsequently restated and strengthened in the 1993 Education Act. Under this legislation a Code of Practice on the Identification and Assessment of Special Educational Needs[42] was introduced to provide more careful and consistent monitoring procedures prior to the initiation of any formal assessment of a child's needs.[43]

While the 1981 Act has been criticised for its retention of a 'discourse on disability', Fulcher has argued that the Act:

> defines special education as provision; in the context of a state apparatus this means resources in general. . . . The Act establishes a generalist discourse and provides a basis for negotiating over and focusing on, resources rather than examining the educational and social context in which particular 'needs' might emerge.[44]

The definition of 'needs' in any given situation may arise from negotiations taking place between people with differing, and sometimes conflicting, interests (those of teachers, parents, other pupils, the LEA and the LEA's professional advisers, for example). However, the Act ignores the role of conflicting interests in the construction of individual needs, focusing solely upon the needs of the child once present. Consequently, the child's needs become the focal point for parallel negotiations between all interested parties over the allocation of resources. Yet this may inhibit the development of a theoretical framework within which the interplay of interests and needs can be examined.[45] The development of an appropriate framework revolves around three questions:

1 Under what conditions is educational disadvantage or 'failure' reconceptualised as 'special educational needs'?
2 Whose needs are defined at that point?
3 How does the power to define the needs of others affect the way the issue of 'special educational needs' is understood?

The 1981 and 1993 legislation treats these questions as unproblematic. The fundamental role of categorisation as a tool for managing resources is ignored. Yet, the upsurge in statements of special educational needs in the 1990s, particularly for 'moderate learning difficulties' and 'emotional and behavioural difficulties', suggests that struggles around these questions impact strongly upon the construction of policy as practice. The logic of replacing categories of handicap with a general and relativistic concept of special educational needs would be to move towards curricular responses rather than organisational or bureaucratic responses. In practice, categories are frequently recreated both as a resource management mechanism by local education authorities and as a tool for prising additional resources out of the system by schools and, increasingly, by organised parent groups.

The politics of 'inclusion'

Looking back from the present day, the Warnock Report may appear to have been an anachronism, even before it was published. The fact that it was commissioned in 1974 by Margaret Thatcher, the incumbent Secretary of State for Education, is not without irony. Post-war optimism about the potential of education for engineering social reform had already begun to splutter, even before James Callaghan's call for a Great Debate challenged belief in a society guided by the rationality of professional technocracy and benevolence. By 1981, a new era had already begun in which much of the responsibility for Britain's alleged lack of industrial competitiveness was laid squarely at the door of those who had championed the post-war civic project. Education as a vehicle for advancing social justice had given way to 'personal choice' theories.[46] These celebrated the rights of the individual and the role of education as a commodity to be traded in the market-place and to be employed as social capital.

The Warnock Report, with its emphasis upon 'professional judgement', was clearly out of step with the onslaught on teachers that climaxed with the 1988 Education Reform Act. On the other hand, the Warnock Report had advanced the view, later encapsulated in the 1981 Education Act, that special educational needs arise from interactions between children and their environments, including their schools. At the time, advocates of a more integrated system of education saw this viewpoint as supporting reform of mainstream schools to make them more inclusive, which it may indeed have been. It was certainly quite explicitly opposed to child-deficit notions of learning difficulties. Moreover, it did go some way towards recognising the importance of the relationship between power and needs. Yet, it failed to fully acknowledge the powerful role of professional interests in defining needs. In the absence of effective mechanisms for protecting the child's interests where those interests might be in conflict with those of more powerful groups, a child-deficit model of needs was inevitably perpetuated. The labelling of individuals or sections of the community as 'needy' carries with it the implication that they lack the power and/or resources to be self-determining. It reinforces the social power of those who are in a position to define the needs of others.

In other areas, the Warnock Report was more in tune with the changing political agenda surrounding education. In particular, the 'schools failure' discourse[47] implicit in the Warnock Report highlighted the ideological ground upon which debates about education would be focused from that time to the present day: the changing relationship between education and the economy. Economic change gave centre-stage to the role of education in channelling individuals into certain sorts of educational experiences, with certification of skills and credentialism being at the heart of this relationship.[48] The introduction of a competencies-based curriculum into the special school sector was in many respects a mechanistic reflection of what was going on in the mainstream sector of education. Yet, in both sectors, this approach reinforced the centralisation of control over education in the hands of government, together with the expansion of surveillance and control.

The birth of the 'audit society', in which economic accountability lay waste to the social purpose of schooling, opened the doors to cost-benefit analysis as the measure of educational outcomes and the value and effectiveness of schools. Ironically, it also pushed the 'inclusion debate' into the mainstream of policy pronouncements. In his foreword to the government's 1997 Green Paper on special education, the Secretary of State for Education, David Blunkett, argued that the underlying principle of inclusion is that of improving achievement:

> Good provision for SEN does not mean a sympathetic acceptance of low achievement. It means a tough-minded determination to show that children with SEN are capable of excellence. Where schools respond in this way, teachers sharpen their ability to set high standards for *all* pupils.[49]

It is particularly interesting that the language used to talk about 'inclusion' in the Green Paper is that of the market (the saleability of achievement) rather than of the social inclusion of difference and diversity.

A political programme for social and economic inclusion centred upon the value of educational achievement in the market-place resurrected the human capital theory of education and training. Yet, it did little to challenge the inequalities that underpin the exclusion of those with limited exchange-value in the market-place of employment. Human capital theories of education do little to advance the interests of young people and adults with learning difficulties who are increasingly excluded from the labour market.[50] Moreover, the policy rhetoric of inclusion disguises the financial imperatives that are reining in the redistribution of goods and services according to 'need'. In other words, the irony here may be that 'inclusive' education becomes the rhetoric that legitimates the withdrawal of an inclusive, if imperfect, system of social welfare.

Conclusion

In this chapter, it has been argued that the growth of a special system of education for people with learning difficulties has been a phenomenon of the modern period. In part, this has been concerned with the control and management of troublesome populations. But, for most of the twentieth century, this project has been guided by the modernist belief in the possibility of rational management of society and the management of difference through assimilation. The chapter has looked at the development of special education and the continuities between pre- and post-1945. It has been argued that although the post-war social reform movement constructed a radically new agenda that emphasised social welfare and social justice, continuity was none the less retained, with the modernist project of assimilation and ultimately of social control and discipline, within the structures of capitalist society. The subsequent contradictions that were revealed in the rapid expansion of a separate system of special education were embedded in the post-war compromise between the reform movement and the capitalist economy. This compromise retained a differentiated system of education linked to the 'needs' of different social classes.

Special education continued to be concerned with assimilating the most troublesome children within a society perceived to be 'normal'. The movement for comprehensive reform in the 1960s represented the most significant challenge to differentiated education; but it was a movement broken on the back of the economic crises of the 1970s and the restructuring of capitalism in the 1980s and 1990s. From this point onwards, the rhetoric of inclusion became a metaphor for the dominance of human capital over social justice.

Chapter 7

Time, space and the construction of identity

Introduction

Life histories provide complex insights into the struggles of people for identity and empowerment. Experience is an important mediator of policy and it is through experiences and actions that policy can be understood as the product of past struggles, penetrated by the struggles of the present. Of course the lives considered in this book are the lives of people at the margins of society, the lives of those with little or no power to affect national or local policy outcomes. They have not changed the course of special educational policy in the twentieth and twenty-first centuries. Yet, their experiences of subordination and resistance do provide important insights into the development of that policy and its significance in relation to broader patterns of social continuity and transformation.

In this chapter, it is argued that the life stories of people with learning difficulties reveal an ordinariness that is often disregarded in the literature on special education. This ordinariness occurs in spaces within what are often highly structured lives. Their lives reflect a struggle to be 'ordinary' and to define their own 'ordinariness' as part of a community in a world that constructs their identities as extra-ordinary. It is argued that this ordinariness is located in social spaces of resistance within family life, the school, the workplace, the day care centre, etc., or in a combination of these spaces. The chapter explores 'hidden transcripts' of dissent that speak to a struggle for emancipated spaces amidst the controlling power of the institutions of public order. It draws in particular upon Habermas's theorisation of the 'life world' and the 'system' to examine how the life world is defended against the domination of space by instrumental and anti-democratic forces.[1] This theme is explored through three life histories that span the period from 1945 to the present day.

'Hidden transcripts'

The political scientist, James Scott, has argued that often people dare not directly confront those who dominate them and control the means by which their lives are publicly represented. Those who are dominant in their social relations with the less powerful, instil inferiority in the minds of the subordinate through acts of power. Resistance to this power is rarely explicit. Instead, a 'social space' may be created and defended within which dissent can be voiced. Such 'off-stage' behaviour Scott identifies as 'the hidden transcript'.[2] These hidden transcripts represent a critique of the powerful, spoken, as it were, behind the backs of the dominant groups but, none the less, articulating resistance and insubordination. They are normally only revealed in the common discourse which underlies the shared values and experience of subordinate groups. This is the discourse of what Habermas refers to as the 'life world'.[3]

Habermas argues that the life world is a sphere of everyday interactions through which people experience a shared sense of meaning with their families, communities, workmates, school-friends, etc. It is reproduced through communication and forms the basis of cultural reproduction and social integration. The life world stands in contrast to 'the system'. The system comprises the structural forces of the economy and the state that both permeate and regulate the life world. Thus the nature of the life world and the resistance which is embedded in it are also ordered by and within the social structures of society.

Foucault has argued that within modern society space and time have been systematically controlled to ensure discipline.[4] Surveillance operates not only to induce the effects of power but also to make those to whom it is applied clearly visible. Special education, as a set of social and cultural practices, has played an important role in shaping the space and time of the modern world. In the second half of the twentieth century, special education was increasingly used to extend the capacities of the system over the life world. Through the identification of deficits and treatment by technical learning, the special school has taken over those spaces in everyday life in which people managed their own identities by social and political communication and action. Moreover, through this process of assimilating the life world under the surveillance and control of the system the modernist project has been more effectively realised than through the exclusionary practices of the eugenics movement. Dominant ideologies are transmitted not simply within schools but through the social ordering of the education system. Resistance is fragmented by the power of the system to define identities and to constrain communicative action.

Exploration of the life worlds of people labelled as having learning difficulties is suggestive of both the structures of subordination through which the system imposes its social order and the resistance that is articulated through the communicative action of the life world. However, it is important not to see the life world simply as a space in which resistance occurs. The life world may be as much a conservative space as an emancipatory space. The system both confronts and intrudes into this space through its regulation of lives. The life world is a space within which the power and effects of the system can be contested but it is also a space within which subordination may be internalised. Giroux has argued that for resistance to be so defined it must have a revealing function that contains a critique of domination and provides opportunities for self-reflection, self-emancipation and social emancipation.

> To the degree that oppositional behaviour suppresses social contradictions while simultaneously merging with, rather than challenging, the logic of ideological domination, it falls not under the category of resistance but under its opposite, i.e. accommodation and conformity.[5]

The three life stories that follow describe different aspects of the relationship between the life world and the system. They illustrate ways in which the life world provides a space within which the label of 'learning difficulties' is contested and how the life world is itself constructed and defended against the penetration of the system. Yet these stories do not idealise the resistance that takes place within and through the life world. They show how alternative identities may be negotiated through communicative action or denied through the disciplinary power of the system. They highlight the contradictory nature of identity formation and, in particular, how the intrusion of the system into the life world both undermines resistance and reconstructs resistance as subordination.

Joan attended both a mainstream and a special school. Since leaving school she has worked in local factories but is now attending a day care centre for people with learning difficulties. Lucy describes her placement in 'the barmy school' and the impact of this upon her place and identity, initially within her family and subsequently in the workplace. Her story tells of her struggle to resist internalising the label of 'stupid' and how the disciplinary power of the system imposed itself upon communicative action within the life world. Stanley describes the ordinariness of 'remembering' as a weapon in his struggle against the denial of personhood that characterised the institutional ownership of his identity.

Joan

Joan attended a residential special school for children who were identified as educationally subnormal just a few years after the 1944 Education Act was passed.

> 'It were a big school. It used to be a hospital before it were a school. We used to do sewing, painting, football, hockey, billiards, croquet and French cricket. We also did reading and writing things as well. I was there till I was 11 and then I had to leave because it was turned into a Children's Home. I got on well with the teachers and the children but it didn't bother me when I had to leave and come back home. It didn't bother me at all. When I came home I went to an ordinary school. We used to come home at dinnertime and then go back at half past one. We did lots of sports – I like sport – and we did reading and writing and numbers. I used to be pretty good at that. I had to leave when I was 15 and then I went to another [day] special school. I was a bit upset about going at first but I soon settled in when I had made some friends. We did running and ballroom dancing. Mind you, we used to come home at a quarter past three so we didn't have a lot of time in the afternoon. We used to do a lot of reading and writing – 'Janet and John' books. We used to draw pictures and then just put 'This is a dog' and 'This is a cat'. We had tracing paper and we had to draw pictures from the reading book on top of the tracing paper.'

This description of her school life shows the control exerted by the system over Joan as her family life is disrupted and she is moved from one school to another. The final part of this quotation is particularly revealing of how the special school system constituted her identity as a young 'child', even though she was by that time 15 years old.

Since leaving school, Joan hasn't worked, but her life has been a full one. She lives with her mother and father. Like most people, Joan's family life is marked by a mix of ordinary family experiences, happiness and tragedy. She is fully involved in the lives of those around her but it is not her 'needs' or 'difficulties' that are characterised as 'special' within the family.

> 'I've got three sisters and two brothers but one of me brothers died not long since. One of me sisters lives in Blackpool. I go there three times a year to see me sister. We have lots of children coming round to the house. We're always babysitting. We have three of them coming on Friday to sleep at our house. One's 6 and the other's 4. Michael hasn't got no mum. His mother died when she was giving birth. He's my brother's boy.'

There is no sense of inferiority in her relations with her family, no sense of being treated differently, no sense of being of less value. That isn't how her family life is. The normalcy of it all isn't an outcome of policies on inclusion, or of professional interventions, or of 'education', or of 'learning support'. It is simply about being part of a family in which she is treated, and treats others, with the same very ordinary dignity and respect as everyone else in that family, unselfconsciously and without effort.

> 'I go shopping with me mum. When we went to town last Saturday there were three joints of meat for £5 so I says, "hey, we'll have some of them". Me mum says, 'what?', and then she spotted it and she says, "hey, I think you're right there". So we had some.'

Joan's social life is similar to her family life in that she both retains considerable control over her activities and refuses to see herself in terms of labels that others might apply. On Monday nights Joan goes to the 'Monday Club'.

> 'A lady comes and picks us up in a minibus and takes us to do ballroom dancing and stuff like that. We are going to the pub next Monday.'

On another night of the week she goes to bingo with her mum.

> 'We have a cab to take us up and down because near where I live there's lots of drugs and you've got to be careful.'

In the daytime Joan spends time at three different Centres.

> 'At Willowbank I do baking, rock climbing, computer surfing, darts, dominoes, draughts. At Moorhouse I do reading and writing and maths and stuff like that and at Brookdale I do embroidery and pottery and we do some macramé.'

For the most part Joan enjoys the different activities and being involved in the Centres. Occasionally things go less smoothly and her ordinary life is troubled by the extraordinary ways in which others treat her and construct her identity as different and threatening.

> 'Up to a while ago I went to the tech but it got a bit iffy if you know what I mean. There was a lot of trouble and we were stopped from going. There was a lot of trouble with other people. They said they didn't want us there and all that.'

Joan's story is not about her 'competence' in managing herself. The notion of 'competence' suggests that there is some standard which a person must reach to be recognised as fully human, but Joan is not measuring herself against others. Nor does her story talk of a life defined by experiences of oppression. Her story speaks rather to the common humanity of a life that we all share. It is a life that is different as all lives are, but at the same time, it is an ordinary human life in which we can recognise common experiences, common feelings, and common problems. Within her life there are moments of subordination, such as her unwilling transfer to a special school, which highlight the dominance of the system in controlling the parameters of her inclusion in society. On the other hand, at key moments, Joan has found the space within the life world of her family and community to define her identity in ways that resist the dominance of those same structures.

The radicalism of her resistance lies in a refusal to accept the definition and consequent constraints placed on her by the system. This is expressed, in particular, through the communicative space of her family relationships where she retains a degree of power in relation to the spatial and temporal horizons of the system. Yet, her resistance is confined to the lived experience of 'ordinariness'. It does not reach beyond this to directly challenge the authority of the system. To this extent, her resistance is personalised and conformist. She expresses her resistance in and through a life world that suggests an alternative way of being but does not articulate a means of politically challenging the authority of the system.

Lucy

Lucy attended mainstream infant and junior schools until the age of 11.

> 'Then I had to go to a special school because I were behind with me work and me mother thought I got picked on a lot because I couldn't keep up with the others. I was bullied and made fun of because people used to call me stuff. It weren't that I couldn't do it, it was just that I took me time to do it.'

The system impacted upon Lucy's life, not just through the decision to send her to a special school when she was 11 but, perhaps more importantly, through the construction of her identity as different and inferior within the mainstream school. Bullying came both from other pupils and from 'a couple of teachers who weren't very nice'. These teachers called her 'slow', 'lazy' and 'stupid'.

The value placed upon school work separates 'ability' from other human attributes and communicative interactions. These system values were internalised by Lucy's classmates, at least in the sense that she was a scapegoat for their own devaluation within the system. In consequence it was not simply Lucy who was disciplined into subordination by the system but also the life world of the classroom. The system imposed itself through socially constructed notions of ability and reward systems that perpetuated myths of success, to fragment the life world and undermine resistance to hierarchical systems of social order.

On leaving primary school Lucy was sent to a local day special school.

> 'In that day and age other people made fun of you saying it were the "barmy school". Children on the street made fun of me. I used to get picked on a lot in the ordinary school. I weren't very good at sticking up for myself then but I started to stick up for myself when I went to special school. I just toughened up if you like.'

Her placement in a special school provided Lucy with the space in which to 'toughen up'. It introduced her into a new life world of people with whom she shared a common identity of subordination.

However, attending special school also had its impact on Lucy's position in her family.

> 'There were eight of us in our family, four boys and four girls. I were the only one who went to a special school out of my family. It felt strange and me dad were a bit strict. He used to call me "stupid" and that 'cos I couldn't keep up with the others.'

In the family, as with the school, the disciplinary control of time and space by the system was focused not solely, or even principally, upon Lucy herself but upon the life world which might give rise to resistance. Whereas Joan found the space within her family life to form a resistant identity, Lucy was further isolated and subjected to the disciplinary power of the system over the family. An immediate consequence of this for Lucy was the impact it had upon her health.

> 'I had a nervous breakdown when I were about 13. I ended up in hospital. Me mum and dad used to fall out a lot and we lost a brother when he was 8 years old. And then there were the change of schools as well. A lot of things worried me. I went to this school when I was 11 and I started to get ill then. I went into hospital when I were 13, on a psychiatric ward and I were there for a long time on and off. I didn't like what was happening. They didn't deal with me problems. All they did were do me up with drugs all the time. That affected me in a lot of ways. When I were in hospital I lost a lot of school and I think that's why I got so far behind.'

Lucy's total isolation and subordination at this stage in her life are not indicative of her exclusion from society, however. Quite the opposite. The central argument of this book is that the role of disciplinary surveillance and control at this time was 'inclusionary'. The system, by ordering and controlling her space to be different, is concerned with assimilating that difference: that is, with normalising and depoliticising the significance of difference for suggesting the possibility of alternative configurations of the social world.

Resulting from these early experiences 'of people calling me stupid and barmy and that', Lucy, like Joan, was determined 'to show them what I can do'. The humiliation of being picked on as different and less than normal ironically gave Lucy a courage and determination to be an ordinary person that has stayed with her throughout her life. As such, her identity is both resistant and conformist. Her resistance is articulated in the representation of her life as 'normal'. She is critically aware of how her difficulties with learning are socially constructed and not explained by personal deficits. On the other hand, she lacks the power and communicative space to reformulate her identity and human value in ways that directly challenge the link between human value and narrowly constructed notions of 'ability'. In this sense her resistance is expressed at the level of the personal not the political. The space within which her resistance takes place is a personal space and not a political space. Her resistance is disconnected from any broader political critique and action. Similarly, she is deprived of participation in those broader communicative spaces that might support political resistance across different but common forms of subordination.

The special school provided the personal space in which to construct her resistance.

> 'I got help at school. It was a slower pace and I think the teachers were understanding.'

It also offered some opportunities to challenge the dominant gendered identities of that period.

> 'We did pottery and woodwork. Even girls had to learn how to do woodwork.'

The main thing about school was that it was 'safe'. Like many children in her position, she found special school to be preferable to the ordinary school because it provided respite from the bullying that she experienced as a matter of course in the ordinary school; but in other ways it isolated her and inhibited opportunities for developing herself.

> 'I've learnt more since I left school. . . . I ended up going to evening classes. I wanted to do better at reading and writing so people wouldn't make fun of me so much.'

Yet, having been labelled as 'subnormal' at school, this label continued to exert disciplinary power over Lucy's life.

> 'Being at special school still has a bad effect even when you've left. When I started work lasses at the factory made fun of me because I went to a special school. I stopped telling people what school I'd been to because I felt ashamed that I'd been there. I used to think, if they know what school I've been to they're going to think I'm stupid; that I'm thick because I went to a special school. You get labelled, don't you.'

This disciplinary power became part of the life world in which she participated, impacting also upon those who did not carry the label of 'learning difficulties'. The depoliticised 'normalisation' of difference through assimilation inhibited the construction by communicative action of a political critique of the disciplinary power that subordinated both Lucy and her workmates. In particular, the scapegoating of Lucy within the workplace stood in the way of any analysis of the role of the factory itself as a unit of disciplinary organisation and control over the lives of all those working there.

Lucy's isolation emphasised to her the importance of the personal politics of resistance. The struggle not to internalise the label of 'stupid' was central to Lucy's sense of self. For her, any differences between herself and others were unremarkable, yet she was keenly aware of how the labels placed on her by her schooling worked to dehumanise her in the eyes of others.

> 'I felt like if you go to a special school people label you as someone who can't do things. Some of them think that if you're backward you're slow and dibby in your brain, but it doesn't mean that. I've been determined to show people that I can do things but I used to think that because someone went to a clever school and I went to a special school that I wasn't as clever as them. But it doesn't mean that. It just means that I had to take more time, that's all. But some people who went to the clever school made fun of me and it can be very hurtful.'

Looking back:

> 'I would say that in some ways school helped me to get confident 'cos it was a slower pace but when I were going for jobs I thought, why aren't they giving me a chance? Do you think that happens to a lot of people what's been to a special school? I mean, I know there are more special schools these days – *there has to be, doesn't there*. But they weren't very caring.'

Stanley

In the late 1930s, Stanley was taken into a children's home following the death of his parents:

> ''cos, you know, when you lose all your parents they were looking for a way to shove me in there.'

Shortly after this, however, he was assessed as 'low grade feeble-minded' and transferred to a hospital. He received no education and, by his own account, minimal care. In describing his early life, Stanley talked of the abuse that inmates endured and the totalising control exerted over the lives of those incarcerated there.[6] He was a child within an adult institution. He had no contact with the world outside the hospital. There was no space for resistance and no place where he could find release from his misery.

> 'It was all men. All hospital beds. Cold. Right in the most bleak part. Right up on the moors. They used to lock the doors. They hit people. They used to lock people in and I didn't like it. You could never go out yourself and pop anywhere on your own. Not anywhere. They locked people in. It used to be staff all the time.'

Having been placed in the hospital he was to remain there for many years. The fact that he received no schooling is almost certainly a consequence of being assessed as being ineducable because of 'severe learning difficulties', but Stanley has no recollection of this. The institution not only defined who he was, i.e. 'retarded' and 'useless', but it also obliterated all other possibilities.

> 'I can't remember things when I was in them places. I've lost all remembering.'

When Stanley talks here of 'remembering' he is not talking literally of his memories of the past but rather of the stripping away of his human identity. His memory of 'helplessness' and 'uselessness' in those years remains very strong.

In the 1980s, he was released from long-term institutional care, not because his mental abilities had in any way improved but simply because the new policy of care in the community had led to the hospital he had lived in all these years being closed. At first, he was placed in council-run residential care but, when that closed down too, he was transferred to a council-run half-way house and started attending a day care centre for the learning disabled. From the half-way house he moved into sheltered accommodation, after being assessed as capable of independent living.

As a child in the 1940s, Stanley had been assessed as ineducable and he had been institutionalised for most of his life. He was now in his late fifties but suddenly, and ironically, rather than learning difficulties being 'revealed' by changes in society, we see new competencies being 'revealed' by policy changes that have 'recategorised' people like Stanley as suitable for independent living. Throughout his childhood, Stanley was considered to be 'ineducable' and for most of his adult life he was viewed as incapable of participation in society. However, Stanley is now living independently, supported only by the warden at his block of flats, a social worker who visits from time to time, and attendance at a day care centre to which he travels by bus.

The intention here is not to make a case for the policy of 'care in the community' as against other policy interventions directed towards people with learning difficulties. There can be little doubt that for Stanley the policy of 'care in the community' has provided him with opportunities for greater independence and control over his own life. On the other hand, for many people community care has meant reductions in public expenditure on care and the privatisation of local authority services through the introduction of a 'mixed economy' of care. Many people with learning difficulties in the community live within a kind of cultural prison of constant poverty and social control.[7] Similarly, the impact of care in the community has not meant for Stanley that his life is free and untroubled. The policy of care in the community is rooted in the downturn of the economy in the 1970s, together with the new political climate of anti-statist, anti-welfare, neo-liberalism that came into ascendancy during the 1980s. The label of 'learning difficulties' continues to operate as a mechanism for imposing social conformity. The needs and opportunities of those to whom this label is applied are still largely externally defined and constrained by their perceived intellectual deficits.[8]

Yet for Stanley, his release from long-stay institutional care has created new spaces within which he has been able to contrast his years in institutional care with his new-found independence in terms of the coming alive of his memory. 'Remembering' is a word he again uses to signify his own sense of identity:

> 'It's only since I've lived here [his own house] that I can remember things. I couldn't even read and write but now I can and I'm doing ever so great with jobs like reading and writing and going to college. I've got a flat. I've got a key of my own which means I can go out and I can go shopping and I'm quite happy with what I'm doing and when I'm on my own I can concentrate, you know like reading and writing.'

In recounting these experiences, Stanley evocatively captures that which the novelist Kundera talks of when he says, 'The struggle of man against power is the struggle of memory against forgetting.'[9]

The stifling of Stanley's identity was a stifling of his ability to be ordinary. The extraordinariness of his experience as a child and young adult lay in the totality of his exclusion from ordinary life – denied the most basic of human rights, abused by 'imprisonment' for 'daring to be different' because of the death of his loved ones and the 'measurement' of his mind as impaired.

His confinement was symbolic of his exclusion from humanity as well as defining the concrete circumstances of his oppression. His lack of memory is an articulation of his extraordinariness, a metaphor for non-existence within society. The regaining of memory is symbolic of his survival. It is a remembering not only of what is in the present but also of the past. Most importantly, remembering has become for Stanley a critical tool, articulating through his reflections on both the past and the present his resistance to the 'imaginary geographies' that cast him as 'imperfect'.[10]

Conclusion

In this chapter, it has been argued that life histories reveal how the development of the system of special education has restricted the life world of people defined as having 'learning difficulties'. The three life stories that have been told give some insight into different aspects of this process. In particular, they have illustrated how struggles within the life world provide opportunities for articulating resistance that is both more effective and politically more conscious. They also show how the life world is penetrated by the system and how, through the label of learning difficulties, the system reconstructs its structures of subordination within the life world of people on whom this label is placed. Moreover, it has suggested how, by setting up social divisions based upon artificially constructed categories of difference, the system reproduces these structures of subordination as disciplinary mechanisms in the life world more generally. None the less, for the people whose stories are told in this chapter, spaces of resistance were generated in their lives by their experiences and social interactions that politicise their dissent. The insights their stories reveal can inform a socio-political critique, not only of the subordination of people with learning difficulties but also of the character of and relationship between different structures of subordination within our society. This argument will be pursued in Chapter 8 where the meaning of 'citizenship' will be explored and consideration given to how this is contested in the lives of people labelled as having learning difficulties. It will be argued that these stories provide important insights into the politics of everyday life.

Chapter 8

Citizenship

Introduction

The boundaries of 'citizenship' that mark levels of participation in society are highly contested, not merely in the disputes of philosophers but also in the day-to-day spaces and places within which battles for social and cultural inclusion and exclusion are fought. For those who seek to cross these boundaries and express the rights of citizenship, the practical restrictions, located both in the structures of the social system and in assumptions about the value of their lives, can be considerable. Such restrictions apply to many individuals and groups, not just those defined as having 'learning difficulties'. The experiences of people with 'learning difficulties', however, do offer important insights into the nature of the negotiations that determine participation and the rights of citizenship.

The distinction between the formal entitlements of citizenship and the capacity to exercise these rights is important.[1] It emphasises the social relations of power that underpin 'citizenship' and forms of participation in society. In considering the citizenship of people with 'learning difficulties' it is necessary to start from an understanding of how the term 'learning difficulties' is itself socially constructed. In this chapter, it is argued that because the label of 'learning difficulties' is a mechanism for managing and controlling a 'troublesome' minority, people with 'learning difficulties' encounter significant difficulties in their attempts to advance their civil rights.

This chapter begins by considering the relationship between citizenship and human rights. It is argued that the concept of human rights is an abstraction that individualises rights and that by doing so promotes dominant social interests. This is contrasted with the concept of 'civil rights' which, it is argued, are the outcomes of practical struggles over power. This theme is further explored through life stories and a critique is put forward that questions the ways in which education has ironically become a metaphor for disempowerment and the disciplinary management of the lives of 'troublesome' people. Finally, the chapter considers how people labelled as having 'learning difficulties' have fought back against the denial of citizenship and how, through politicised dissent, they challenge dominant conceptualisations of the constitution of democracy in our society.

Citizenship and human rights

It is often assumed that citizenship is dependent upon a concept of a person that incorporates autonomy, rationality and the faculty of making choices and entering into agreements. On the basis of this model of citizenship, people identified as having 'learning difficulties' have at different times and to different degrees been excluded from citizenship. People with 'learning difficulties' have been denied the right to vote, the right to form relationships, the right to bear and raise children, the right to work, the right to live in the community, and so on. Decisions have been made about people that have imposed disciplinary authority over the body (as in the case of sterilisation and the denial of free movement) and over the mind (as in the denial of choice in respect of education and controls exerted over participation in political organisation through self-advocacy). The rights of citizenship have been constrained by the representation of people with 'learning difficulties' as 'childlike' or as less than human.

The model of citizenship outlined above is grounded in the individualism of the Enlightenment philosophy of the eighteenth and nineteenth centuries. John Stuart Mill, in his famous essay 'On Liberty', argued that a natural antagonism exists between political authority and the individual. The state is understood as a force that interferes with, and limits the freedom of, the individual. And although some form of social cohesion is provided through the state it is important to restrict the role of the state to the barest minimum. For this reason, there is need of regulation of the power of the state by reference to fundamental philosophical principles.[2] It is contended that the rights of citizens are sanctioned by natural law. Locke maintained that at the basis of social order was the proposition that individuals are entitled to respect as moral agents capable of choice.[3] This model represents citizenship in terms of the rights of the individual against the political authority of the state. Human rights are said to be inalienable and guaranteed to the individual within the political community. Citizenship is therefore derived, in Rousseau's terms, from a 'social contract'[4] and is located in its defence of individual freedom in the face of the Hobbesean jungle of competing interests.[5]

The concept of human rights is not unproblematic. One problem with this way of understanding citizenship is that it ignores the socially constructed character of autonomy, rationality and choice, as well as the socially constructed character of labels that signify the absence of these supposed attributes of the citizen. Its location in abstract philosophical principles masks its own grounding in the particular social and economic relations. The philosophy of human rights reflected the rising power of a capitalist class and its demands for de-regulated trade and the maximisation of individual preferences.[6] The philosophy of human rights was therefore a political articulation of the aspirations of a rising social class that already controlled economic power but was politically restricted in exercising this power by an anachronistic old regime. The philosophy of human rights was concerned with establishing the conditions of social and political freedom that would optimise the economic possibilities for this bourgeois class.

By contrast, classical liberalism had little to say about the rights of workers against the power of capital, although it was keen to emphasise the inalienable right of workers to sell their labour. Similarly, the rights of people who were destitute, ill, insane, 'feeble-minded, etc., and whose lives were dislocated by the new domination of the capitalist mode of production, were of little or no concern to a capitalist class seeking to gain political power for itself. Only when the power of the capitalist class was consolidated by its ascendancy within the apparatus of the state did concerns about maximising the efficiency of those on the margins of society become an issue. Yet, devoid of any analysis of the historical and social context within which the interests of dominant groups impacted on subordinate groups in constructing their needs, the notion of human rights poorly articulates the experiences of those subordinate groups in society.

By abstracting the concept of rights from real historical and social contexts, they are reified, disarmed and divorced from the resistance of everyday life and the continuous struggle between contending social interests. While articulated as an abstract principle, the concept of rights is limited in its impact and in particular may be constrained within the bounds of an ethical critique of exclusion which offers no strategies for bringing about change. As an ethical critique, the language of human rights inadequately problematises the relations of power and control that underpin the construction of interests of some as the 'needs' of others. The language of rights obscures not only their political origin but also the antagonism between different social interests.

A distinction might usefully be drawn between human rights that are a reflection of self-interest and political or civil rights that can only be exercised in common with others. From the latter perspective, rights must be understood in the context of the specific power relations that underpin them, a context that comprises both cultural and historical aspects as well as interpersonal and institutional aspects. Through their day-to-day experiences, people are brought face-to-face with the social hierarchies that keep them subjugated within the 'rational' social order. In turn this encourages resistance to the social order of capitalism and opens up possibilities for alternative forms of social organisation and reconceptualisations of the rights of citizenship. Outside of the formal, institutional contexts within which people are defined in the deficit terms of 'learning difficulties', such disabling contexts often contrast with other 'safe havens' such as the family, the workplace, the self-advocacy group, social clubs, friendship groupings, etc., in which alternative understandings of citizenship are negotiated and established.

In so far as the needs of different people and of different socially, culturally or biologically defined groups are understood as different and, in certain cases, as special, conditions of dependency are created. Assumptions about the qualitative nature of such differences both mask and reinforce the political and social practices by which repressive forms of power and control are exercised and legitimated. Alternatively, human needs may be understood within a framework that emphasises what they have in common, in which case it is the absence of the conditions that satisfy those needs, rather than the character of needs specific to particular individuals or groups, that must be the object of investigation and the target of change.[7]

Citizenship, participation and exclusion

Citizenship is a highly contested concept. It is defined and re-defined in the social negotiations of everyday life, as well as by the broader principles embodied in legislation and social policy. Each of the stories described in Chapters 3 to 5 illustrates how, at different stages in the history of special education, people experienced exclusion because they were given the label of 'learning difficulties' (or its earlier formulations as 'feeble-mindedness' and 'mental retardation', etc.). For each of them, the labelling process constituted a defining moment with far-reaching implications for their lives, reflecting in different ways their subordination and the regulation of their lives within society. Moreover, schooling was a key arena in which future participation or its absence was imposed or negotiated.

Over the last two hundred years, the label of 'learning difficulties' and its earlier variants ('idiot', 'feeble-minded', 'mentally deficient', 'subnormal', etc.) have been imposed on increasing numbers of people. New technologies of assessment were developed and used to identify increasing numbers of 'mentally deficient' people for treatment in asylums, hospitals, schools, colleges, and specialist centres built to contain or rehabilitate those considered to be 'troublesome', economically inefficient, or having 'special needs'.

These policies, in part, reflected the growing sophistication of the political system and the ability of social reformers to influence policy outcomes within the context of an increasingly mature capitalism that demanded differentiation and regulation of the labour force. They also reflected the contradictions that ensued from the development of capitalism and the rational organisation of society. Capitalism demanded an economic order based upon individualism and the production of profit. Maximisation of profit required a potential workforce that was disciplined and fully assimilated within a homogeneous social system. The unnecessary exclusion of sections of the population from this potential workforce was inefficient. In consequence, attention was drawn to the possibility of more finely differentiating between those who were educable and therefore potentially available to work and those who were not.

Copeland has argued that the idea that there is 'a continuum of mental weakness or deficiency',[8] far from being invented by the Warnock Committee, is characteristic of a continuing policy tradition in respect of special education. This tradition goes back to the Egerton Commission which had concluded that 'there is no clear line separating idiots and imbeciles: it is merely a difference of degree, not of kind. Idiocy means a greater degree of deficiency and imbecility means a lesser degree of such deficiency.'[9] Similarly, the term 'feeble-minded' was 'applied to children who are too mentally defective to be properly taught in ordinary elementary schools, but not so defective as to be imbecile'.[10] The crucial factor was 'the ability to earn a living'.[11] Moreover, in distinguishing feeble-minded children as a distinct class which should be educated separately, the Egerton Commission was following the precedent of the earlier Cross Commission on elementary education which maintained that such children were no longer 'to be regarded as "ordinary children"'.[12]

This was a tradition that was to become established in the continuity of special educational policy for the next hundred years. The number of children labelled as mentally defective steadily rose during the first half of the twentieth century from 5,672 in 1903–4 to 13,651 in 1913–14.[13] By 1939, the number of children 'ascertained' as mentally defective had risen to 17,000.[14] The post-war reforms pursued the policy of identifying people with 'learning difficulties' and treating them in separate schools or classes with a new vigour. By 1976, some 53,772 children were being taught in separate schools for the subnormal, with a further 13,064 attending ESN classes in ordinary schools.[15] However, as argued in Chapter 6, the downturn of the economy at the end of the 1970s, together with the new political climate of anti-statist, anti-welfare, neo-liberalism that characterised the 1980s and 1990s, brought with it a policy agenda of 'inclusive education' and 'care in the community'.[16]

This policy shift led to major changes in the lives of people with 'learning difficulties'. As argued in Chapter 7, the introduction of a 'mixed economy of care' forced many people with learning difficulties into a 'cultural prison' of poverty and social control.[17] On the other hand, the development of de-institutionalised service provision has encouraged recognition of the importance of service user perspectives in the evaluation of provision.[18] In so far as the policy of community care required the views of people with 'learning difficulties' to be taken into account, service providers as an integral part of the service delivery process promoted self-advocacy groups for people with 'learning difficulties'.[19] However, the fundamental relations that produce 'learning difficulties' as a form of social oppression remain unchanged.

The evaluation of services may be informed by the views of users, but those who define the goals and outcomes of service provision continue to be professionals. It is professionals, not users, who manage services and who identify the recipients of the provision. Moreover, the label of 'learning difficulties' continues to operate as a mechanism for imposing social conformity. The participation of users in the evaluation of services doesn't in any fundamental way challenge the outcomes of being defined as 'learning disabled'. The needs and opportunities of those to whom this label is applied are still externally defined and constrained by their perceived intellectual deficits.

Experiencing citizenship?

The experience of people with 'learning difficulties' tells us that citizenship is neither an attribute nor a right but is rather a social relation that is defined by the boundaries that specify inclusion and exclusion. In this section, I want to draw on two examples to illustrate how citizenship is experienced, denied and contested in the lives of people with 'learning difficulties'. Both examples highlight uses of 'education' as a means of control but also show how this control is resisted by those involved by their attempts to negotiate their citizenship rights.

Penny

Penny attended the special needs class of a local further education college. During her first year at college she had been taking basic education classes but the year was coming to an end and she had been discussing with her tutor, Dave, the sort of courses that she might be able to join in the following year. Penny wanted to join a one-year full-time catering course in the ordinary college. She had gained experience of cooking at school and it was one of the things she liked to do at home, frequently helping to cook meals for the family. Penny thought that the qualifications and experience she would gain from a 'proper' course would help her get a job, possibly in a residential home for the aged. She had already had a successful work experience placement in the kitchen of this type of home and enjoyed working with and supporting elderly people.

> 'I went to see my tutor about the course but he doesn't want me to do it. He wants me to go on a course that's only one day a week. It's all people from the special school. That's not what I want to do but he'll probably get his own way.'

Penny didn't feel in control of this situation. She didn't question that her tutor was trying to act in her interests but the bigger question was that of who was defining her interests. She clearly saw that she was being pushed in a particular direction and that this was happening not just because of *her* circumstances and needs but rather because *this was what people from the special school have to do*. Her future was not being decided on the basis of a consultation about her needs in which her views were central to the outcome. The decision seems instead to have been based on the expectations that professionals have about people with 'learning difficulties' and the provision that has been put in place to match those expectations. Yet, this was not the end of the story for Penny because next she tried to negotiate her participation on the catering course in the ordinary college by directly approaching the tutor for that course.

> 'Me mum and me talked to the woman who takes the course and she was all right about it but she said that she would talk to Dave. You know he's going to talk to her and try and persuade her that it will be in my best interests to do one day a week. I'm going to ring her to see if I can do full-time and then go down to one day a week if I find it too hard. Well, I'm going to try my best to get – well not my own way but the upper hand and get what I want to do.'

This act of resistance was an important articulation of Penny's claim to citizenship. The catering course tutor was sympathetic but Penny was very aware of the weakness of her position. Even with her mother's support, she recognised that because she has been labelled as having 'learning difficulties' the catering course tutor was not going to make a judgement without reference back to the special needs department. Unlike most of us, she wasn't going to be given the opportunity to succeed or fail in her chosen career because the label made the career choice an 'unsuitable' one. It is also interesting to see how Penny's mother was marginalised in the decision-making process because of the label of 'learning difficulties' attached to her daughter.

> 'What's important to me is not important to him. He just wants me to do what he thinks is best for me. Because I'm in this centre it's difficult to get into a main course and get what you want. It wasn't even discussed at all whether I wanted to be in a mainstream situation or a separate situation. That's what I would have liked. I would have liked them to discuss and ask me: "Would you like to have a go in mainstream, then if you find that you can't do it, go and see the Assisted Learning Centre." What I mean is students should have rights to be able to be listened to. Just to be listened to and not to be fobbed off all the time.'

Penny was able to articulate the thoughts and feelings that other people might find more difficult to find words for and she made a strong case. Those less able to articulate their citizenship in this way would very likely have been even more disadvantaged. None the less, the label itself disempowered Penny, like others who carry this stigma. Penny's frustration with this situation was apparent when she compared her own experience of being denied participation in 'normal' society with that of her sister who does not carry the label of 'learning difficulties'.

> 'I mean, my sister wasn't treated like that and she went to mainstream. She wasn't treated like that at all. I mean, it just makes me sick the way they treat normal students better than they treat us. They don't get treated as though they're kids or as though they're thick but we do and they get listened to, they get their ideas or suggestions listened to but we don't and things like that. Normal students, if they've got a lesson and they don't want to do it, they can just go to the canteen and not get told off about it. If we do that we get an absolute rollicking.'

Penny gave no hint of using the phrase 'normal students' in a way that would suggest 'internalised oppression'. It was used to characterise the way she and other people in similar situations to herself are made different by the imposition of labels. Indeed, it is very striking that Penny's experiences of being denied the rights of participation and citizenship and her struggles to contest this on a regular basis have probably given her a more acute sense of the nature of citizenship than many of us have. Lessons were learnt about denial, about the power of authority to make decisions over whose voices are to be valued, about resistance and about the importance of resistance to self-respect, even when resistance seems futile.

Contesting citizenship through self-advocacy

The second example I want to explore in this chapter, which illustrates the way in which citizenship is contested and negotiated, focuses upon the experience of people with 'learning difficulties' in the mushrooming self-advocacy movement. Self-advocacy for people with 'learning difficulties' has its origins in the Swedish leisure clubs of the 1960s that were run by the members themselves. Out of these early activities developed the first 'Swedish National Conference of Retarded Adults' which met in 1968. From this the movement quickly spread to different parts of the world. [20]

These early self-advocacy groups were characterised by the activity of individuals and groups, who in the past had experienced individual and/or collective disempowerment. People with 'learning difficulties' were speaking out for change in their lives, and social welfare organisations and professionals were, for the first time, being made to listen to this previously ignored group of people.

A number of people who were involved in the research for this book were active in the self-advocacy movement and saw it as having the potential to offer a stable, safe context for the development of meaningful relationships which are self-created, in contrast to community care settings organised by others. For Donna:

> 'It helped me being in a self-advocacy group because my friends help me to stick up for myself. When my friends are down I help them. When I am down they help me.'

Similarly, for Gary, 'we all listen to each other and we help each other and get things done'.

Bob, a group supporter who himself has 'learning difficulties', defined the aims of his group in terms that were politically more overt.

> 'The aim . . . is to stamp out all forms of discrimination and to encourage people with learning difficulties to speak up for themselves and to take up services but only if they have been changed. To encourage people with learning difficulties in everyday life.'

This statement provides a political articulation of the views of many other group members who recognised the importance of supporting each other in the face of the discrimination experienced in their everyday lives. In this respect, Bob's statement echoed the views of Williams and Shoultz who, in writing about the political significance of self-advocacy, emphasised the importance of acknowledging the previous life histories and experiences of people with 'learning difficulties'. They offer respect and admiration for the courage it takes to stand up for themselves, for, historically, they are one of 'the most devalued, neglected and abused groups in society'.[21] To challenge traditional views of themselves against authority, institutions and people's attitudes takes courage. Williams and Shoultz include a political dimension to their definition that suggests the possibility of real change. They write that: 'Self-Advocacy means self-respect, respect by others, a new independence, assertiveness, and courage. It involves seriousness, political purpose and understanding of rights, responsibilities and the democratic process.'[22]

The changing policy agenda towards care in the community for disabled people, however, has encouraged the growth of service-based self-advocacy groups. Whereas groups such as People First are associated with the demand for people with 'learning difficulties' to be heard, to make choices and to exercise civil rights, free of those labels that legitimate discrimination and disempowerment, service-based self-advocacy groups have been set up by professionals to focus on practical strategies within the human service industry to de-institutionalise people with 'learning difficulties'. In other words they are a mechanism for evaluating service systems.[23] A survey of adult training centres documented the growth of self-advocacy in this sector and this is a trend that points to the fit between self-advocacy in service bases and the user participation and community care discourses in government policy that have come to the fore since the mid-1980s in Britain.[24]

Despite the rhetoric that surrounds 'user participation' and service-based advocacy, disabled people themselves often feel the opportunities for taking control over their own lives to be heavily constrained by the desire of service providers to set up provider-led mechanisms for user evaluation of services. Simone Aspis argued that in these circumstances, 'Self advocacy has become a tool to find out what people with learning difficulties think of services rather than to challenge the philosophy of services and systems that create them and their inherent limitations.'[25] Moreover, within these contexts, 'self-advocacy has become concerned with supporting individuals to gain "realistic" change within institutions by using inter-personal skills valued by professionals without challenging their status and power'.[26]

Undoubtedly, contemporary demands for innovative methods of 'user participation' have intensified professional and policy-maker interest in self-advocacy as a potential context for empowerment in action.[27] Professionals involved in supporting or encouraging self-advocacy frequently break down the idea of 'speaking out' by examining the areas they think will be affected – relationships, opportunities, independence, self-confidence, self-image, and decision-making. They look at the skills, the support and the teaching that may be needed to realise the 'advocates'' full potential. Sometimes the components they see making up the concept of self-advocacy are echoed by members of self-advocacy groups, but professional definitions and discussions often fail to include, or do not give enough recognition to, the life experiences of people with 'learning difficulties' and their views of the world.

In reality, the service-based model of self-advocacy may also contribute to the institutionalisation of that experience and to the fragmentation of political action through the colonisation of the 'voices' of people with 'learning difficulties'. Professional voices can easily mask the complex, heterogeneous, hierarchical and conflicting collection of individuals and groupings that are to be found within self-advocacy groups. Professionals speaking for people with 'learning difficulties' can do so in subtle and not so subtle ways, but when this occurs it may emphasise values that are alien but which assume a homogeneous grouping with easily discernible needs and objectives. However, rather than being a 'given', a political and value consensus within a self-advocacy group is more likely to be constructed through complex negotiations which take place within the context of hierarchical formations and power relations.

The following example illustrates the complex negotiations that take place around citizenship within service-based self-advocacy groups. This particular group was based in a day centre for adults with 'learning difficulties' and was supported by the service provider. An issue that greatly concerned this group was the appointment of staff to the centre. The local authority had a policy of involving users in the appointment of staff. As part of the staff appointment procedure, users interviewed applicants. The views of users were then fed back to the management group by a carer, and this latter group (which independently interviewed applicants for posts) made decisions about appointments. The users of this centre had a keen interest in contributing to the decision-making process and emphasised the significance of the role of their self-advocacy group as a means of giving them some control over the operation and activities of the centre. However, the group was frustrated by the fact that the applicants they supported were frequently not appointed.

In this example, there are actually two forms of 'citizenship' in operation. In the first of these forms (that employed by the local authority and its service managers), citizenship is based upon a concept of a person that incorporates autonomy, rationality and the faculty of making choices and entering into agreements. On the basis of this model of what it is to be a citizen, the involvement of people identified as having 'learning difficulties' in the decision-making process through the centre's self-advocacy group is seen as educational. One might ask, of course, 'educational to what end?' Is this process one that will, through the accumulation of skill and experience, lead to full citizenship, or is education being used to legitimate the denial of citizenship and to mark the relations of power and control in society that underpin this denial? In the absence of the power to enforce citizenship as a right, the notion of citizenship becomes not only a sham but also a system of control. In this sense, the discourse of citizenship is a bogus discourse. Yet this is not the whole story.

To focus only upon the disempowerment of people in this context is to present a very one-sided view (a view that in itself contributes to the continuing oppression of certain social groups by their representation only as victims). *In practice citizenship and control are consistently being contested in the daily lives of these centre users.* We find, therefore, a second, unofficial, form of citizenship in operation. It is evidenced, for instance, by the insistence by members of the group of their right to participate as 'citizens' through the collective actions of the group in contesting the meaning and extent of their citizenship. To 'roll over' and accept the artificiality of their citizenship would, for the members of the group, be to be complicit in their own oppression. Instead they use the opportunities that are provided by the interviews to assert the significance of issues that are important to them in the appointment of support workers. The fact that members of the group are aware of the boundaries that have been placed around their 'citizenship' and yet use the group to contest these boundaries flies in the face of the purpose of the group as perceived by the management committee of the centre that established the group in the first place. This is not, therefore, simply an illustration of a service-based self-advocacy group being used to confuse and disempower its members (although this is certainly part of the story). It suggests also how the structures that are used to define and control the citizenship of group members are contested and subverted in practice as they attempt to redefine their citizenship.

The point is not simply that the group is oppressed and denied citizenship by the structural forces that socially construct 'learning difficulties' in certain ways. It is rather that, in contesting the limits of citizenship, the group also contests the definition and operation of citizenship in political practice. Thus, a citizenship practice is constructed through the actions of the group, not so much by their assertion of independence (which at best is partial), but through an ongoing struggle that challenges the socially constructed character of 'autonomy', 'rationality' and 'choice' and the socially constructed labels that signify the absence of the attributes of citizenship, e.g. 'learning difficulty', 'mental retardation', and other such labels. Self-advocacy, in this context, is characterised not by the formal structures of the group, but rather by the collective struggle for a meaningful citizenship in opposition to the control that is exerted over group members through the structures of the service-based self-advocacy group.

The role given to the day centre self-advocacy group in the above example is a role that 'normalises' the exclusion of its members as non-citizens. By contrast, the members of the group contest this process of exclusion through their understanding that all people are entitled to be respected and have the right to participate in society. The problem faced by members of the group in this example does not arise merely because the institutional context structures their activities and hence their marginalisation. Self-advocacy, in this context, also operates to confine and isolate the political activities of its members, while normalising a perspective on citizenship that traps people with 'learning difficulties' in a world of 'training to become', but never fully participating as, citizens. Aspis has argued:

> It remains the case that it is not in the interests of many of those who claim to support us to provide this particular kind of support because it would change the power balance in the relationship between us and them and would mean different structures and ways of working which bear no resemblance to those to which they are accustomed.[28]

Conclusion

The self-advocacy movement represents in microcosm some of the fundamental issues and struggles that characterise a democratic citizenship. As Barton argues, citizenship is a terrain of struggle and, in recognising this, 'we need to understand the nature and extent of the exclusionary processes involved and their differential impact on the lives of particular individuals and groups'.[29] Far from being a state of *being*, 'citizenship' is perhaps better understood as a process of *becoming*. As such, it is continually being contested and negotiated in social practice. It is concerned with the endeavours of individuals and groups to participate on equal terms and with dignity in the life processes of which they are a part. This is not only about political struggle. It is also about belonging and being accepted on terms that are fair, humane and dignified. At times the relationship between these is not always clear, and the struggle for 'rights' may seem to conflict with other more tangible qualities of citizenship. As one self-advocate put it:

> 'I used to be a member of loads of committees fighting for rights and all that . . . yeah, and the disability Movement do some great stuff for other people. But how's all that stuff on politics going to get me a girlfriend and a job.'

An appreciation of different and diverse 'voices' is important for any understanding of the way civil rights are constructed and denied in the everyday social practices of life. These voices are important not because they are representative of an experience that is unique but rather because they give expression to a struggle for civil rights and citizenship. Moreover, in speaking and hearing of these struggles it becomes possible to share in what is common across our differences and thereby to explore new forms of common struggle. Citizenship must be defined not simply in terms of equality of participation but also by actions, both individual and collective, of all those who struggle for their own participation. In this sense, explorations into the citizenship of people with 'learning difficulties' become an exploration into the notion of citizenship itself.

Chapter 9

Seizing the future by recapturing the past

Breaking the culture of silence

This book has considered the development of special education policies since the end of the Second World War and has advanced the argument that a life-historical perspective illuminates the contested values and interests that have been struggled over in the growth of the special education sector in the UK. Moreover, it has been maintained that life stories are grounded in the wider social, economic and political processes of society. They both reveal the operation of these structures and illustrate the nature of resistance to them. For example, 'inclusion' has been a major theme of recent policy debates in education, but this concept is not an abstract principle. It is a policy discourse that is politically defined in different ways at specific historical moments. Thus, as taken up by the disability movement, it can articulate a socio-political critique of oppression, while in other contexts it may describe policies of economic retrenchment and depoliticised social normalisation.

The weakness of much policy analysis in the field of special education has been that it has failed to engage with the voices of disabled people and others who have been labelled as having 'special educational needs' or 'learning difficulties', and so on. People's experiences of special education open up new ways of thinking about the politics of exclusion and inclusion. Historical analysis needs to take these voices seriously for they challenge both the homogeneity of experience and the social relations that have constructed difference as 'abnormal'.

In this final chapter, it is time to pull together the different elements of the argument advanced in the book and to consider the future of special education and, in particular, the prospects for 'inclusive education' within a society rapidly moving into a new phase of its development. I will begin by summarising the argument put forward in the book about the relationship between social inclusion and modernity. Second, I will consider the question: 'Does inclusive schooling have a future?' Third, I will argue that systems of regulation, together with evidence of resistance to such forms of social control, reveal 'cracks in contentment'. These illustrate the structures of the system and the forms of opposition that are articulated within the 'life world' of everyday experience. Finally, I will argue that a useful comparison can be made between the experiences of people whose life stories are described in this book and Freire's analysis of the 'culture of silence' in respect of colonial domination of developing countries. Policy has itself been an important component in creating a culture of silence because it implies something that is done to others. Breaking the culture of silence requires political solutions that extend democratic participation to those whose voices have been silenced.

The 'civic project' of inclusion

It has been the contention of this book that the 'civic project' of 1945 attempted to draw the boundaries of social inclusion in ways that assimilated all sections of society. Educational provision was characterised by a framework that provided differentiated schooling focused on the separate needs of different social classes and groups. This reflected continuation of a model of social life that was rooted in the Enlightenment. Enlightenment thinking emphasised the freedom of individual action but placed it within the context of a rational social order. It was this belief in the rationality of the social order that maintained a balance between the competing pressures of individual expression and innovation on the one hand and social coherence on the other. It also provided the optimal conditions in which preferences and choices within the market-place could be exercised, thus allowing the development of capitalist modes of production to proceed unfettered by traditional social bonds.

Inclusivity, under conditions of rational control, was central to the idea of modernity. It was the glue that stuck capitalism together. It was a necessary corollary to the freedom of the market. There were three reasons for the importance of social inclusion to the development of capitalism. In the first place, social inclusion maximised the potential market-place for goods and therefore profit. The second reason for the importance of inclusivity was that it maximised the efficiency of labour, while minimising the drain of the poor on the state. Thirdly, it regulated social order through disciplinary systems that were constituted by the structures and relations of social participation, including schooling.

By contrast, policies of social exclusion, although of continuing significance throughout the nineteenth and early twentieth centuries, were concerned with those on the margins of this system of order. Eugenicists advocated segregation and isolation of the 'feeble-minded', but the underlying rationale of this movement was focused on 'human improvement' rather than simply on the exclusion of the undesirable. As the twentieth century progressed, the technology of assimilation made the politics of exclusion redundant. Schools, for example, were refined to meet the needs of different kinds of children, and professional knowledge became increasingly sophisticated in measuring fine differentiations of ability and aptitude.

The post-war election of a Labour government with a large majority in Parliament did provide a tremendous impetus towards a more radical redistribution of wealth mediated through the state. The creation of a welfare state represented a significant break with the past in that it put an explicit concern with providing for the needs of disadvantaged individuals and groups at the centre of social and educational policy. Yet, this willingness to use the state to intervene in promoting social well-being did not extend to offering a socialist alternative to capitalist relations of production. The impetus of social and educational policy remained focused on a narrowly defined notion of participation in the labour force: namely, that of equipping people with the skills to contribute to the community, itself still defined in terms of an economy that was capitalist. Policy continued to be concerned with the demarcation of those people who could participate in the labour force from those who could not.

Thus, in the post-war period the twin aims of social policy became rehabilitation and welfare, both of which were based upon the values of social responsibility and inclusion. Support for those who it was judged could make a useful contribution to society was based more firmly than in the past upon the idea of rehabilitation. Support for those who were judged to be incapable of self-support was provided on the basis of compassion and collective social responsibility. The welfare state thus reflected continuity with the nineteenth-century distinction between the 'deserving' and 'undeserving' poor. It fell far short of the socialist ambition of redistribution on the principle, 'from each according to his means to each according to his needs'. The latter would have required not only steps towards socialising the distribution of wealth, but also socialisation of the means of wealth creation. In maintaining the inequities of private ownership, it was inevitable that entrenched inequities in the value placed upon different citizens would also remain. People with 'learning difficulties' were not liberated, but were silenced by assimilation.

The integration of disabled people as citizens of 'normal' society was a goal to be realised through the philosophy of rehabilitation, but only on condition that they could be assimilated within the boundaries that defined that society's normality. As Henri-Jacques Striker has argued:

> Now, those who were formerly disparate and objects of the acts of the kind-hearted do have rights but they are named with a specificity that constitutes an identifying marker. Moreover, if we examine the rights that have been accorded them, they are only those that all citizens have and that have never been the object of formal declaration: the right to work, the right to education, the right to a guaranteed economic life, and so on. For the disabled, these rights are stated, promulgated. . . . The disabled, henceforth of all kinds, are established as a category to be reintegrated and thus to be rehabilitated.[1]

This post-war period was the high point of the modernist project. It represented a triumph of social inclusion that at one and the same time signalled the inclusiveness of society and the dominance of social inclusion as a mode of disciplinary control. Yet, it was a dream that was to be shattered at the end of the twentieth century. Boundaries of exclusion were redrawn, as capitalism awoke from its own dependency on welfare support from the state to usher in a new reality of individualism, diversity, and the commodification of need.

By the last quarter of the twentieth century, traditional distinctions between the market and social welfare were breaking down. Capitalism exploded into new markets, reducing social relations in all cultural settings, including education, to the exchange relations of the market-place. The costs of social welfare were now seen as a crippling burden by government. Education policy became a key site on which the battle to redefine the purposes, outcomes and costs of welfare was to be, and still is being, fought.

Government initiatives introduced in the 1980s and 1990s changed the face of educational policy. Yet, by the late 1990s, there were still some 1.6 million children identified in the UK as having special educational needs, and in excess of £350 million was being spent annually by local authorities on special education.[2]

> The modernized comprehensive system now sanctioned selection and differentiation, the education market encouraged schools to avoid or exclude children who were difficult to teach, an increasing number of parents were claiming entitlement to extra resources for their statemented children, all of which meant higher costs. The government faced the 150-year old dilemma over the costs of educating young people who might not be economically profitable to the society and who did not fit into a human capital equation.[3]

This was the context in which the inclusion debate came to be at the centre of education policy in the late 1990s.

Does inclusive schooling have a future?

This ideological shift of the 1980s and 1990s impacted on special educational provision in two ways. In the first place, resources became more hotly contested. As resources were shifted from local authorities to schools under the provisions of local management of schools (LMS), there was a significant reduction in LEA-managed support services. Yet, a lack of financial regulation and accountability in respect of schools' non-statemented special educational needs budgets led to concerns that the overall budget allocated for special education within the mainstream sector was effectively being reduced as schools diverted this money into other areas.[4] Ironically, in the 1990s government commitment to reductions in public expenditure resulted in more pressure being exerted for access to the greatly reduced resources retained by LEAs. Thus, the number of statements for special educational needs (together with the additional resources that followed them) continued to rise at a significant rate throughout the 1980s and 1990s.[5] In consequence, LEA professionals such as psychologists were placed more than ever at the front line of budgetary control – managing resources rather than supporting learning.

In the second place, the professional ethic of service came under increasing pressure as the agenda for reform in education shifted away from that set by the liberal theories of consensus which had underpinned the philosophy of the Warnock Report. These were now replaced by a new orthodoxy of consumer-driven market forces.[6] The reforms of the new regime struck at the heart of teachers' professional autonomy as a 'schools failure' discourse replaced the humanitarian benevolence of the post-war 'special needs' discourse.[7] Teachers were held responsible, and publicly blamed, for the failure of pupils to achieve standards set by government. Professional services were subjected to the discipline of the market-place, with consumer (parental) choice becoming the arbiter of quality, and the state coming in as enforcer through its new inspection regime.[8]

The devolution of resources from LEAs to schools gave control over financial planning to a new managerial bureaucracy within schools, but it was accompanied by the centralisation of policy-making in the hands of the Department for Education and Employment and the Treasury. External pressures were brought to bear on schools and teachers to adopt pupil selection and financial policies to maximise their competitiveness in the market-place. Thus, a raft of policy initiatives over recent years has demarcated, and pumped additional resources into, selected schools as centres of excellence whose pupils are distinguished by their special aptitudes and abilities. The supposed failure of comprehensive education was given as the justification for this retreat from inclusion.[9] In these circumstances, the very presence of large numbers of children with special needs in mainstream schools, particularly where those needs were linked to learning and/or behaviour difficulties, was seen as harmful to a *school's* performance on national curriculum tests. This was a powerful force for exclusion.

Ironically, debates about educational equality and inclusion have continued to take centre-stage at the very time that educational policy has noticeably moved in a very different direction. Comprehensive education might be rapidly becoming a thing of the past. There may be a preoccupation with technical solutions to educational issues as the transformatory role of education has been neutralised by a narrow focus upon competencies and performance. None the less, as Tomlinson argues, 'New Labour was possibly more open and pragmatic about SEN dilemmas than previous governments.'[10] Recent policy initiatives around 'inclusive education' for those children identified as having special educational needs may be seen as bucking this trend. It has certainly been the case that the rhetoric of inclusion has featured strongly in the two most significant policy statements of the New Labour government on special education.[11] But even here it could be argued that rhetoric has masked the ways in which increasing numbers of children are being formally identified as having 'learning difficulties' (for instance through the Code of Practice on Special Educational Needs).[12] Perhaps, as Jock Young has argued, we have entered into a new phase of an exclusive society that is much more ready to accept differences, but also more ready to exclude, and 'exclusion is based not on difference but on risk'.[13]

In the latter part of the twentieth century, special education has been extended to increasing numbers of children as well as adults. This has taken place at a time when the economy has gone through the restructuring of de-industrialisation and many people have been excluded from the labour market, partly because their skills are now redundant and partly because of the inflation in qualifications required for even the most menial of jobs. The education system is now faced with the problem of how to provide schooling for young people who are increasingly denied access to the labour market and unlikely to make an economic contribution to society.

There were and are many pressures within the system that encourage the use of special education procedures to exclude troublesome children and the use of special schools as a means of managing those children once excluded.[14] Moreover, special education has become a convenient mechanism for legitimating the discriminatory management of other 'social problems'. For example, special education has played an important role in constructing racialised notions of intellectual inferiority and problem behaviour. We have been aware of racialised decision-making in education at least since Bernard Coard wrote, in the early 1970s, about how the West Indian child is made educationally subnormal in the British school system.[15] Numerous studies since that time have confirmed the position of black children as more likely to be placed in a special school,[16] more likely to be excluded from school,[17] more likely to be placed in the care of the local authority,[18] and more likely to be convicted of a crime,[19] than their white classmates. Despite this research evidence, little has changed. Special educational needs is a convenient tool for legitimating discrimination, racism and the lack of opportunities in general for young people.

Special educational needs may also be invoked to delegitimate the child's voice.[20] This was the case for Penny, in Chapter 8, whose attempt to gain a placement in a mainstream college was thwarted by the label she had been given. Other life stories discussed in this book illustrate this point. The label of 'learning difficulties' operated as a powerful mechanism of control upon the lives of those who experienced the system of special education in the third quarter of the twentieth century. Yet, there are clear indications that young people are now finding it much harder to break free from the effects of this label through social and economic participation. The inadequacy of the policy framework of special educational needs, and of a professional practice defined by that framework, for dealing with issues of discrimination, is one that disempowers children and adults with 'learning difficulties'. It also, inevitably, de-skills teachers and other professionals who work with them. It does so because it inhibits genuine partnerships based on an understanding of the way children themselves experience the world.

Regulation and resistance

In this book it has been argued that special education is a regulatory system. The life stories provide insights into the development of the system of special education. They also illustrate how resistance to this disciplinary system is expressed. But regulation and resistance are not necessarily two separate things. The one penetrates and critiques or reinforces the other. As sociologists have long maintained, the greatest power of regulation lies in the internalisation of its systems as part of the 'normal' experiences and activities of everyday life.

In Chapter 7, life stories were explored to illustrate and unpack these processes, drawing in particular upon the theoretical insights of Habermas's discussion of the 'life world' and the 'system'. It was argued that the system reproduces and institutionalises social divisions as a disciplinary mechanism. It is a mechanism that is highly effective. One important sense in which regulation is effective is in its disciplinary impact upon those who do not bear labels such as 'learning difficulties'. The stigmatisation of difference reinforces conformity among the 'normal'.

Resistance, however, is generated in the social relations of our lives. A functionalist theory of regulation would have us all as obedient and docile. In reality, the struggles of everyday life bring confrontations with the system that force us to make choices about who we are and the kind of life that we want. For the most part, these choices are not ones that fundamentally challenge the authority of the system to regulate our lives, but they express, as Okely argues, the 'cracks in contentment' that illustrate the structures of subordination experiences (see Chapter 2).

Citizenship, as was argued in Chapter 8, is a part of life around which identities are hotly contested and, for people defined as having 'learning difficulties', most radically disputed. The label is a metaphor for the absence of citizenship rights. Resistance, however, is often not so much a choice as an inevitable outcome of 'normal life'. It is often simply an expression of the desire for an identity. The institutionalisation of people with 'learning difficulties' in the early part of the twentieth century denied, almost totally, the possibility of an independent identity. The growth of special education in the late twentieth century, linked to a programme of assimilation or normalisation, brought with it a contradiction. Special education was designed to promote participation. But, at the same time, the labels that it created were markers of deficiencies that legitimated the denial of citizenship. Those who have been part of that system struggle with this contradiction every day of their lives. Resistance is most importantly about self-respect. It is often concerned with no more than the struggle for participation in what is 'ordinary'.

The nature of the regulatory process, its impact upon people with 'learning difficulties', together with the resistance that is expressed, also exposes the broader social structures of regulation in society. This is a web of disciplinary control that holds us all. Although the struggles of individuals to free themselves from that web are rarely successful in breaking its clutches, acts of resistance to the system, such as those described by many of the contributors to this book, are politically significant in what they reveal about the system. From their own experiences of resistance, many people with 'learning difficulties' are now joining together to raise a collective voice through the self-advocacy movement. Even this has its pitfalls, and like other forms of collective political action self-advocacy can be colonised, diverted and silenced. But this movement does point to a way forward and does suggest how the day-to-day struggles of everyday life can politicise and be politicising in ways that strengthen resistance and present alternative forms for organising the social relations of our society.

Self-advocacy is a beginning. It provides a space for different voices to be heard and for the strength of collective struggle to be experienced. Beyond this lie alliances with others who experience these struggles in different ways. But, there is an important question that comes out of the history of resistance by people with 'learning difficulties', and that is: 'What do these histories tell *me* about *my* own history and *my* future?'

Breaking the 'culture of silence'

Freire has discussed the character of the dependency of the underdeveloped world on the first world in terms of a 'culture of silence':

> The culture of silence is born in the relationship between the Third World and the metropolis. It is not the dominator who constructs a culture and imposes it on the dominated. This culture is the result of the structural relations between the dominated and the dominators. Thus, understanding the culture of silence presupposes an analysis of dependence as a relational phenomenon that gives rise to different forms of being, of thinking, of expression, to those of the culture of silence and those of the culture that 'has a voice'.[21]

This argument is relevant not only to an understanding of the relationship between first world and developing countries but also to the relationship between different social interests within those countries.

In arguing that the social relations of power play an important role in constructing, mediating and silencing different voices, it is not being argued that all experience or all knowledge claims are equally valid as truths about the world. Nor does Freire suggest that certain social interests, because of their political, social and economic dominance, are able to simply impose their version of events or the superiority of their knowledge claims. Even less does Freire make the empiricist claim, recast in postmodernist clothes, that knowledge is the product of experience and that therefore different experiences give rise to different forms of knowledge.

What Freire does maintain is that to understand the culture of silence is to understand the hegemonic relation between social interests by which the partiality of truth (that is, belief in the necessity of certain 'truths') is revealed as a mutual relationship that enforces dependence. He argues that the inequality between voices is a reflection of the structures of knowledge production: that is, of the forms of power relations between peoples. The voice of dominant social interests is expressed through the social structures that enforce the dominance of these interests.

Speaking one's own history, therefore, is a crucial step towards liberation from the constraints that the labels of subordination have imposed. These labels have meaning precisely because they signify subordination. To challenge them in speaking of one's own history is to create the space for alternative understandings. It is to seek out alternative ways of seeing the world, and alternative ways of theorising the origins and continuing importance of systems for classifying human beings into categories of people who lack the intelligence or the competence, or whatever it is that is deemed to be in deficit.

Freire argues that:

> Only when the people of a dependent society break out of the culture of silence and win their right to speak – only, that is, when radical structural changes transform the dependent society – can such a society as a whole cease to be silent toward the director society.[22]

The stories of people with 'learning difficulties' speak volumes to their disempowerment and to the denial of their voice in decisions relating to their lives. Yet, the social interests of more powerful individuals and groups are not simply imposed, they are also internalised, and it is in challenging the internalisation of subordination that the role of history is fundamental to a reconstruction of the future.

If, as Barton maintains, inclusion involves 'listening to unfamiliar voices, being open, empowering all members and [is] about celebrating "difference" in dignified ways',[23] then the struggle for inclusion remains far from won. The contention of this book has been that hearing these voices is not just about creating spaces for stories of resistance to be spoken. It demands that the culture of silence be broken. This can only be done by making connections across the biographies that separate us, to challenge the structural forces in society that operate upon our lives. It demands recognition that the label of 'learning difficulties' is not a description to be applied to people but a category that disenfranchises people from participation in society as valued and equal citizens. To speak and to listen, is to rename the struggle for policy reforms as a political struggle for a common programme of social emancipation.

Notes

Introduction

1 U. Beck, *Risk Society: Towards a New Modernity*, trans. Mark Ritter, London: Sage, 1992.
2 I. Culpitt, *Social Policy and Risk*, London: Sage, 1999. D. Lupton (ed.) *Risk and Sociocultural Theory: New Directions and Perspectives*, Cambridge: Cambridge University Press, 1999. J. Young, *The Exclusive Society: Social Exclusion, Crime and Difference in Late Modernity*, London: Sage, 1999. H. Kemshall, *Risk, Social Policy and Welfare*, Buckingham: Open University Press, 2002.
3 F. Galton, *Hereditary Genius, its Laws and Consequences*, London: Macmillan, 1869. A. Tredgold, 'The feeble-minded: a social danger', *Eugenics Review*, 1909, vol. 1, pp. 97–104.
4 Department of Education and Science, *Special Educational Needs* (The Warnock Report), London: HMSO, 1978.
5 S. Tomlinson, 'The expansion of special education', *Oxford Review of Education*, 1985, vol. 11, no. 2, pp. 157–165. B. Norwich, *Segregation Statistics*, London: CSIE, 1994.
6 T. Booth, 'Challenging conceptions of integration', in L. Barton (ed.) *The Politics of Special Educational Needs*, London: Falmer Press, 1988. T. Booth, 'Inclusion and exclusion in England: who controls the agenda?' in F. Armstrong, D. Armstrong and L. Barton (eds) *Inclusive Education: Policy, Contexts and Comparative Perspectives*, London: David Fulton, 2000, pp. 78–98.
7 G. Fulcher, *Disabling Policies: A Comparative Approach to Educational Policy and Disability*, Lewes: Falmer Press, 1989.
8 F. Armstrong, 'The historical development of special education: humanitarian rationality or "wild profusion of entangled events"?' *History of Education*, 2002, vol. 31, no. 5, pp. 437–450.
9 R. Porter, *A Social History of Madness: Stories of the Insane*, London: Phoenix, 1996, p. 3.
10 Statutory regulations made under the provisions of the 1944 Education Act specified eleven 'categories of handicap', one of which was children who were 'educationally subnormal'. The 1970 Education (Handicapped Children) Act brought a further group of previously 'ineducable' children into the fold of special education and thus the category was subdivided into groups deemed to have moderate and severe subnormality – ESN(M) and ESN(S). In 1981 the Education Act of that year replaced 'categories of handicap' with a generic category of 'special educational needs'. In practice, however, the term 'learning difficulties' continues to be used to refer to children previously categorised as subnormal, as well as more

generically to all children with special educational needs. In the former case children tend to be labelled by the type of special educational provision they receive, either as having 'severe' or 'moderate' learning difficulties.

11 D. Armstrong, *The Life Histories of People with Learning Difficulties* (Final Report to the Economic and Social Research Council, Grant No. R000221555), Swindon, ESRC, 1998.

1 The menace of the 'other' within

1 H-J. Striker, *A History of Disability*, trans. William Sayers, Ann Arbor, Mich: University of Michigan Press, 1999.
2 Ibid., p. 33.
3 Ibid., p. 35.
4 M. Foucault, *Madness and Civilization: A History of Insanity in the Age of Reason*, London: Tavistock, 1967.
5 Striker, op. cit., p. 69.
6 Ibid., p. 79.
7 Foucault, op. cit.
8 Ibid., p. 13.
9 Ibid., p. 16.
10 Ibid., p. 26.
11 Ibid., p. 35.
12 Ibid., p. 36.
13 Striker, op. cit., p. 85.
14 Ibid., p. 85.
15 M. Foucault, *Discipline and Punish: The Birth of the Prison*, London: Peregrine Books, 1979.
16 S. Tomlinson, *A Sociology of Special Education*, London: Routledge and Kegan Paul, 1982. S. Tomlinson, *Educational Subnormality: A Study in Decision-Making*, London: Routledge and Kegan Paul, 1981.
17 Tomlinson, 1981, op. cit., p. 31.
18 J. Hurt, *Outside the Mainstream: A History of Special Education*, London: Routledge, 1988.
19 A. Gramsci, *Selections from the Prison Notebooks*, London: Lawrence and Wishart, 1971.
20 G. Sutherland, *Ability, Merit and Measurement: Mental Testing and English Education 1880–1940*, Oxford: Clarendon Press, 1984.
21 Ibid.
22 Quoted in D.G. Pritchard, *Education and the Handicapped 1760–1960*, London: Routledge and Kegan Paul, 1963, p. 117.
23 W.W. Ireland, *On Idiocy and Imbecility*, London: J. & A. Churchill, 1877.
24 Sutherland, op. cit.
25 H.H. Goddard, *Feeble-Mindedness: Its Causes and Consequences*, New York: Macmillan, 1914.
26 Ibid., pp. 2–3.
27 Ibid., p. 558.
28 Tomlinson, 1982, op. cit.
29 Sutherland, op. cit., p. 157.
30 Ibid., p. 157.
31 Board of Education, *Report of the Mental Deficiency Committee* (The Wood Committee), London: Board of Education, 1929.
32 Striker, op. cit., p. 85.

33 J. Duncan, *Mental Deficiency*, London: Watts & Co, 1938, pp. 87–88.
34 Ibid., pp. 2–3.
35 Ibid., p. 2.
36 S. Tomlinson, 'The expansion of special education', *Oxford Review of Education*, 1985, vol. 11, no. 2, pp. 157–165.
37 Ibid., p. 157.
38 Ibid., p. 164.
39 S. Tomlinson, 'Why Johnny can't read: critical theory and special education', *European Journal of Special Needs Education*, 1988, vol. 3, pp. 45–58: 48.
40 J. Ford, D. Mongon and M. Whelan, *Special Education and Social Control: Invisible Disasters*, London: Routledge and Kegan Paul, 1982.
41 J. Finch, *Education as Social Policy*, London: Longman, 1984.

2 Whose history is this?

1 J. Ryan and F. Thomas, *The Politics of Mental Handicap*, London: Free Association Books, 1987, p. 85.
2 G. McCulloch and W. Richardson, *Historical Research in Educational Settings*, Buckingham: Open University Press, 2000, p. 17.
3 M. Oakeshott, *Experience and its Modes*, Cambridge: Cambridge University Press, 1933, p. 99. For a discussion of historical idealism see also E.H. Carr, *What Is History?* London: Penguin, 1964.
4 R.G. Collingwood, *The Idea of History*, London: Oxford University Press, 1961.
5 H. Silver, *Education as History: Interpreting Nineteenth and Twentieth Century History*, London: Methuen, 1983.
6 Ibid., p. 21.
7 S. Ball, *Education Reform: A Critical and Post-structural Approach*, Buckingham: Open University Press, 1994, p. 16.
8 D. Atkinson, M. Jackson and J. Walmsley, *Forgotten Lives: Exploring the History of Learning Disability*, Plymouth: BILD, 1997. P. Morris, *Put Away*, London: Routledge and Kegan Paul, 1969.
9 P. Murray, unpublished PhD, University of Sheffield, 2003.
10 J. Dewey, *Philosophy, Psychology and Social Practice – Selected Essays*, New York: G.P. Putnam's Sons, 1963.
11 G.H. Mead, *Mind, Self and Society*, Chicago: Chicago University Press, 1934. H. Blumer, 'Society as symbolic interaction', in A.M. Rose (ed.) *Human Behavior and Social Processes*, Boston: Houghton Mifflin, 1962; H. Blumer, *Symbolic Interactionism*, Englewood Cliffs: Prentice-Hall, 1969.
12 R. Rorty, *Philosophy and the Mirror of Nature*, Princeton: Princeton University Press, 1979.
13 D. Harvey, *The Condition of Postmodernity: An Enquiry into the Origins of Cultural Change*, Cambridge, Mass.: Blackwell, 1990.
14 F. Nietzsche, *The Will to Power*, New York: Vintage Books, 1968.
15 H.S. Becker, *The Outsiders: Case Studies in the Sociology of Deviance*, New York: The Free Press, 1963.
16 E. Goffman, *Asylums: Essays on the Social Situation of Mental Patients and Other Inmates*, London: Pelican, 1968.
17 W.F. Whyte, *Street Corner Society: The Social Structure of an Italian Slum* (3rd edn), Chicago: Chicago University Press, 1981.
18 J.M. Charon, *Symbolic Interactionism: An Introduction, an Interpretation, an Integration*, Englewood Cliffs: Prentice-Hall, 1979.

19 I. Copeland, 'Pragmatism: past examples concerning pupils with learning difficulties', *History of Education*, 2001, vol. 30, no. 1, pp. 1–12.
20 G. Fulcher, *Disabling Policies: A Comparative Approach to Educational Policy and Disability*, Lewes: Falmer Press, 1989.
21 M. Lipsky, *Street-level Bureaucracy: Dilemmas of the Individual in Public Service*, New York: Russell Sage Foundation, 1980.
22 T. May, *Reconsidering Difference*, University Park, Pa.: Pennsylvania State University Press, 1997.
23 S. Best and D. Kellner, *Postmodern Theory: Critical Interrogations*, New York: Guilford Press, 1991.
24 M. Foucault, *The Archaeology of Knowledge*, London: Tavistock, 1972.
25 Ibid., p. 172.
26 See also T.S. Popkewitz, B.M. Franklin and M.A. Pereyra, 'Preface', in T.S. Popkewitz, M.A. Pereyra and B.M. Franklin (eds) *Cultural History and Education: Critical Essays on Knowledge and Schooling*, New York: RoutledgeFalmer, 2001, pp. ix–xiii.
27 T.S. Popkewitz, M.A. Pereyra and B.M. Franklin, 'History, the problem of knowledge, and the new cultural histories of schooling', in Popkewitz *et al.*, op. cit., p. 13.
28 Popkewitz, Franklin and Pereyra, op. cit., p. ix.
29 Ibid., p. x.
30 B.M. Franklin, *From 'Backwardness' to 'At Risk': Childhood Learning Difficulties and the Contradictions of School Reform*, Albany: State University of New York Press, 1994.
31 Popkewitz, Pereyra and Franklin, op. cit., p. 25.
32 Franklin, op. cit., p. xii.
33 A. Gramsci, *Selections from the Prison Notebooks*, London: Lawrence and Wishart, 1971.
34 In 'The poverty of philosophy' (T. Bottomore and M. Rubel, *Karl Marx: Selected Writings in Sociology and Social Philosophy*, London: Penguin, 1963, p. 195). Marx argues that 'Economic conditions had in the first place transformed the mass of the people into workers. The domination of capital created the common situation and common interests of this class. Thus this mass is already a class in relation to capital, but not yet a class for itself. The interests which it defends become class interests. But the struggle between classes is a political struggle.' See also E.P. Thompson, *The Making of the English Working Class*, London: Gollancz, 1963. Thompson maintained that the making of the working class is a fact of political and cultural, as much as of economic, history. This emphasises the importance of the distinction between a 'class in itself' and a 'class for itself'. Whereas the former is constituted 'objectively' as an analytical category, the latter constitutes itself by its actions. However, post-structuralists, in critiquing the concept of 'class', generally start from the analytical category of 'objective' class interests, ignoring the ways in which those interests are historically defined and made meaningful as social practice by social action and not as the deterministic outcome of the analytical categories themselves.
35 Nietzsche, op. cit.
36 M. Hammersley, *Reading Ethnographic Research: A Critical Guide*, New York: Routledge, 1998.
37 Blumer, 1969, op. cit.
38 For example, see P. Lather, *Getting Smart: Feminist Research and Pedagogy within the Postmodern*, New York: Routledge, 1991.
39 Hammersley, op. cit.

40 McCulloch and Richardson, op. cit., p. 17.
41 P. Lather, 'Fertile obsession: validity after poststructuralism', in A. Gitlin (ed.) *Power and Method: Political Activism and Educational Research*, New York: Routledge, 1994, pp. 36–60.
42 R. Moore and J. Muller, 'The discourse of "voice" and the problem of knowledge and identity in the sociology of education', *British Journal of Sociology of Education*, 1999, vol. 20, no. 2, pp. 189–205.
43 P. McClaren, *Critical Pedagogy and Predatory Culture: Oppositional Politics in a Postmodern Era*, London: Routledge, 1995, p. 197.
44 Ibid., p. 195.
45 A.C. Sparkes, 'Life histories and the issue of voice: reflections on an emerging relationship', *Qualitative Studies in Education*, 1994, vol. 7, no. 2, pp. 165–18.
46 I. Goodson and P. Sikes, *Life History Research in Educational Settings: Learning from Lives*, Buckingham: Open University Press, 2001, p. 17.
47 Ibid., p. 214.
48 C.W. Mills, *The Sociological Imagination*, London: Oxford University Press, 1959.
49 Ibid., p. 214. See also J. Kincheloe, 'Educational historiographical meta analysis: rethinking methodology in the 1990s', *International Journal of Qualitative Studies in Education*, 1992, vol. 4, no. 3, pp. 231–245. Kincheloe argues that educational historians should find new ways to uncover how power is produced and reproduced, how subjectivities are made and how objectivity is defined. This would involve not only an explanation of how certain ideas get legitimated but also tough questioning about the legitimacy of those ideas.
50 J. Okely, *Own or Other Culture*, London: Routledge, 1996.
51 Ibid., p. 214.
52 Ibid.
53 J-P. Sartre, *Being and Nothingness*, London: Routledge, 1989.

3 Lives in special education: disciplinary transitions

1 Board of Education, *Report of the Mental Deficiency Committee* (The Wood Committee), London: Board of Education, 1929.
2 D. Atkinson, M. Jackson and J. Walmsley, *Forgotten Lives: Exploring the History of Learning Disability*, Plymouth: BILD, 1997. M. Oswin, 'A historical perspective', in C. Robinson and K. Stalker (eds) *Growing Up With Disability*, London: Jessica Kingsley Publications, 1998. J. Ryan and F. Thomas, *The Politics of Mental Handicap*, London: Free Association Books, 1987.
3 R. Reiser, 'Disabled history or a history of the disabled', in M. Mason and R. Reiser (eds) *Disability Equality in the Classroom – A Human Rights Issue*, London: Inner London Education Authority, 1990.
4 Atkinson *et al.*, op. cit.
5 Ryan and Thomas, op. cit.
6 E. Compton, *A History of Whittington Parish*, Leeds: The Standard Publishing Company, 1931.
7 'The school was opened in 1878 by four young men. At that time it was surrounded by some of the worst slums in the town but thanks to the efforts of the Corporation the area presented a very different aspect to-day. The school began on Unitarian and undenominational lines and had continued as such right down to the present day. Prior to being taken over as the Ragged School, the building was a public house called the Wagon Inn, and the four founders began their work in a small room above the entrance to what was then known as "The Dog Kennels".' *Derbyshire Times*, 3 November 1923, p. 2.

8 M. Foucault, *Discipline and Punish: The Birth of the Prison*, London: Peregrine Books, 1979, p. 141.

4 Lives in special education: the post-war expansion

1 See, for instance, L.S. Hearnshaw, *Cyril Burt: Psychologist*, London: Hodder and Stoughton, 1979.
2 Ministry of Education, *Handicapped Pupils and School Health Regulations*, Statutory Rules and Orders, no. 1076, London: HMSO, 1945. Ministry of Education, *Handicapped Pupils and School Health Regulations*, Statutory Instruments, no. 365, London: HMSO, 1959.
3 Department of Education and Science statistics for pupils attending ESN schools between 1950 and 1976 show a gender imbalance of approximately three boys to one girl throughout this period. Cited by S. Tomlinson, *Educational Subnormality: A Study in Decision-Making*, London: Routledge and Kegan Paul, 1981, p. 81.
4 Remploy was set up in 1945 in response to the 1944 Disabled Persons (Employment) Act. Its mission statement is 'To expand the opportunities for disabled people in sustainable employment within Remploy and the communities it serves.' http://www.remploy.co.uk/ (accessed 6 October 2002).
5 See S. Tomlinson, 'The expansion of special education', *Oxford Review of Education*, 1985, vol. 11, no. 2, pp. 157–165.
6 The 1970 Education (Handicapped Children) Act repealed section 57 of the 1944 Education Act which had made the Health Service responsible for 'ineducable children'. It was estimated that about 32,750 children were involved. Department of Education and Science, 'The last to come in', *Report on Education, no. 69*, London: HMSO, 1971.
7 Reiser refers to this self-hatred as 'internalised oppression'. R. Reiser, 'Disabled history or a history of the disabled', in M. Mason and R. Reiser (eds) *Disability Equality in the Classroom – A Human Rights Issue*, London: Inner London Education Authority, 1990. This idea builds upon classical labelling theory. For instance, Cicourel and Kitsuse argued that once an individual has been labelled he/she may be expected to live up, or down, to this label. A. Cicourel and J. Kitsuse, *The Educational Decision-Makers*, Indianapolis: Bobbs Merrill, 1963.
8 'The rampant growth and not just blooming institutions . . . is a consequence of the policies of 1945, in particular the celebrated founding legislation of social security . . . based in an effective and proportional solidarity among citizens and in a quite complete and thorough assumption of responsibility for care.' H-J. Striker, *A History of Disability*, trans. William Sayers, Ann Arbor, Mich: University of Michigan Press, 1999, p. 141.
9 See D. Galloway and C. Goodwin, *The Education of Disturbing Children*, London: Longman, 1987.

5 Lives in special education: the management of learning difficulties

1 H. Giroux, *Theory and Resistance in Education: A Pedagogy for the Opposition*, London: Heinemann, 1983, p. 43.
2 Department of Education and Science, *Special Educational Needs* (The Warnock Report), London: HMSO, 1978.
3 Giroux, op. cit., p.109.
4 S. Tomlinson, *Education in a Post-Welfare Society*, Buckingham: Open University Press, 2001, p. 99. S. Tomlinson, 'The expansion of special education', in B. Cosin,

M. Flude and M. Hales (eds) *School, Work and Equality*, Sevenoaks: Hodder, 1989, p. 195.

6 Special education and the politics of educational reform

1 Jock Young argues that there has been a return to the nineteenth-century notion of 'deserving' and 'undeserving' poor. J. Young, *The Exclusive Society: Social Exclusion, Crime and Difference in Late Modernity*, London: Sage, 1999.
2 Z. Bauman, *Thinking Sociologically*, Oxford: Blackwell, 1990, pp. 182–183.
3 Ibid.
4 Ibid., p. 226.
5 Ibid.
6 M. Foucault, *Madness and Civilization: A History of Insanity in the Age of Reason*, London: Tavistock, 1967.
7 The significance of the eugenics movement, and its pseudo-scientific fantasies, in informing the genocides of the late twentieth century cannot and should not be forgotten or understated. It is perhaps through the genocides of modernity that the incestuous logic of self-consuming homogeneity began to implode. The resurrection of these fancies in the form of the new genetics reinforces the main point of my contention. On the one hand, the new genetics is heralded for the possibilities it offers for limiting suffering and improving the quality of life (even by some within the disability movement); it is seen as reducing the chaos of pain. On the other hand, the production of 'designer babies' is also advocated for its 'value' in enhancing the species; in other words, extending, but also narrowing, our parameters of normality. These two viewpoints represent different sides of the same eugenicist coin. In the first case, suffering is understood from the position of 'normalcy'. The meaning of suffering is feared because it represents a chaotic abyss into which any one of us might fall. Suffering is not understood as part of the human condition. It is endowed with neither the fatalism nor the spiritual qualities attributed to it in pre-modern times. The production of life itself is feared for its chaotic unpredictability.
8 G. McCulloch, *Educational Reconstruction: The 1944 Education Act and the Twenty-First Century*, Ilford: Woburn Press, 1994.
9 Ibid., p. 93.
10 Ibid., p. 113.
11 R.H. Tawney, *Equality* (4th edn), London: George Allen and Unwin, 1952.
12 Children with severe learning difficulties were not included within the education system until 1970.
13 Ministry of Education, *Handicapped Pupils and School Health Regulations*, Statutory Rules and Orders, no. 1076, London: HMSO, 1945.
14 Ministry of Education, *Handicapped Pupils and School Health Regulations*, Statutory Instruments, no. 365, London: HMSO, 1959.
15 D. Galloway, *Schools, Pupils and Special Educational Needs*, London: Croom Helm, 1985, p. 29.
16 Department of Education and Science, *Statistics*, vol. 1, 'Schools 1974–1976', London: HMSO, quoted by S. Tomlinson, *Educational Subnormality: A Study in Decision-Making*, London: Routledge and Kegan Paul, 1981, p. 81.
17 J. Goldthorpe, D. Lockwood, F. Beckhefer and J. Platt, *The Affluent Worker in the Class Structure*, Cambridge: Cambridge University Press, 1968.

18 Tomlinson, op. cit., p. 82. See also B. Coard, *How the West Indian Child is Made Educationally Sub-normal in the British School System*, London: New Beacon Books, 1971.
19 E. Powell, 'Like the Roman I see the River Tiber foaming with much blood', speech given by Enoch Powell, 20 April 1968, http://www.sterlingtimes.org/text rivers of blood htm (accessed 7 December 2002).
20 The UK's first Immigration Act was passed in 1971 and came into effect in 1973. This Act, though amended by subsequent legislation, remains the core legislative pronouncement on immigration, defining, as it does, those with the 'right of abode' in the UK and those who do not have this right.
21 Beginning with the Industrial Relations Bill in 1968 and ending with the 'winter of discontent' in 1978 when the Labour Party's 'Social Contract', rejected by its own supporters, was finally, and irreversibly, ditched by capitalism, which in the new global economy had no further need for the politics of consensus.
22 G. McCulloch, *Failing the Ordinary Child?: The Theory and Practice of Working-Class Secondary Education*, Buckingham: Open University Press, 1998, p. 146.
23 Central Advisory Council for Education (CASE), *Children and their Primary Schools* (The Plowden Report), London: HMSO, 1967.
24 Ibid., para. 151.
25 W. Brennan, *Curricular Needs for Slow Learners*, London: Evans, 1979.
26 Tomlinson, op. cit.
27 Department for Education and Employment, *Code of Practice on the Identification and Assessment of Special Educational Needs*, London: DfEE, 1994; Department for Education and Skills, 2001.
28 Department of Education and Science, *Special Educational Needs* (The Warnock Report), London: HMSO, 1978, p. 59.
29 Ibid., ch. 7.
30 D.L. Kirp, 'Professionalism as a policy choice: British special education in comparative perspective', in J.B. Chambers and W.T. Hartman (eds) *Special Education Policies: Their History, Implementation and Finance*, Philadelphia: Temple University Press, 1983.
31 See Chapter 1, this volume.
32 M. Rutter, B. Maughn, P. Mortimore, J. Ouston and A. Smith, *Fifteen Thousand Hours: Secondary Schools and their Effects on Pupils*, London: Open Books, 1979.
33 M. Aglietta, *A Theory of Capitalist Regulation*, London: New Left Books, 1979.
34 V. Pareto, *Sociological Writings*, ed. S.E. Finer, London: Pall Mall, 1966.
35 D. Stone, *The Disabled State*, Basingstoke: Macmillan, 1984.
36 N. Tutt, 'The unintended consequences of integration', *Educational and Child Psychology*, 1985, vol. 2, no. 3, pp. 130–138.
37 D. Harvey, *The Condition of Postmodernity: An Enquiry into the Origins of Cultural Change*, Oxford: Blackwell, 1990, p. 121.
38 Ibid., p. 123.
39 'The point is that the State does not have at its disposal the means of quickly and cleanly cauterizing these contradictions. They can only be solved in ways that lay the seeds of further contradictions. Thus, "buying loyalty" in various ways is fine but the price keeps going up as privileges become rights.' R. Dale, *The State and Education Policy*, Milton Keynes: Open University Press, 1989, p. 31.
40 G. Fulcher, *Disabling Policies? A Comparative Approach to Educational Policy and Disability*, Lewes: Falmer Press, 1989, p. 42.
41 J. Callaghan, 'Speech by the Prime Minister, the Rt. Hon. James Callaghan, MP, at a foundation-stone laying ceremony at Ruskin College, Oxford, on 18th October', Press Release, 1976.

42 Department for Education and Employment, 1994, op. cit.
43 Audit Commission, *Getting in on the Act. Provision for Pupils with Special Educational Needs: The National Picture*, London: HMSO, 1992.
44 Fulcher, op. cit., p. 167.
45 D. Armstrong and D. Galloway, 'Who is the child psychologist's client? Responsibilities and options for psychologists in educational settings', *Association for Child Psychology and Psychiatry Newsletter*, 1992, vol. 14, no. 2, pp. 62–66. D. Armstrong and D. Galloway, 'On being a client: conflicting perspectives on assessment', in T. Booth, W. Swann, M. Masterton and P. Potts (eds) *Learning For All 2: Policies for Diversity in Education*, London: Routledge/Open University, 1992, pp. 193–203.
46 See, for example, the government White Paper of 1992 that proposed disciplining poorly performing schools by allowing parents greater choice over their children's schooling within the state sector. This led to the 1993 Education Act and the setting up of Grant Maintained Schools that would be free of local authority controls. Department for Education, *Choice and Diversity: A New Framework for Schools*, Cmnd 2021, London: HMSO, 1992.
47 D. Galloway, D. Armstrong and S. Tomlinson, *The Assessment of Special Educational Needs. Whose Problem?* London: Longman, 1994.
48 A. Coffey, *Education and Social Change*, Buckingham: Open University Press, 2001, p. 71. F. Coffield, 'Introduction and overview: attempts to reclaim the concept of the learning society', *Journal of Educational Policy*, 1997, vol. 12, no. 6, pp. 449–455.
49 Department for Education and Employment, *Excellence for All Children: Meeting Special Educational Needs*, London: The Stationery Office, 1997, p. 4.
50 S. Riddell, S. Baron, K. Stalker and H. Wilkinson, 'The concept of the learning society for adults with learning difficulties: human and social capital perspectives', *Journal of Educational Policy*, 1997, vol. 12, no. 6, pp. 473–484.

7 Time, space and the construction of identity

1 J. Habermas, *The Theory of Communicative Action: Vol. 1 Reason and the Rationalization of Society*, Boston: Beacon Press, 1984. J. Habermas, *The Theory of Communicative Action: Vol. 2 Lifeworld and System*, Boston: Beacon Press, 1987.
2 J. Scott, *Dominion and the Arts of Resistance: Hidden Transcripts*, New Haven, Conn.: Yale University Press, 1990.
3 Habermas, 1987, op. cit.
4 M. Foucault, *Discipline and Punish: The Birth of the Prison*, London: Peregrine Books, 1979.
5 H. Giroux, *Theory and Resistance in Education: A Pedagogy for the Opposition*, London: Heinemann, 1983, p. 109.
6 See E. Goffman, *Asylums: Essays on the Social Situation of Mental Patients and Other Inmates*, London: Pelican, 1968.
7 P.M. Ferguson, D.L. Ferguson and S.J. Taylor (eds) *Interpreting Disability: A Qualitative Reader*, New York: Teachers College Press, 1992.
8 D. Armstrong, 'The politics of self-advocacy and people with learning difficulties', *Policy and Politics*, 2002, vol. 30, no. 3, pp. 333–345.
9 M. Kundera, *The Book of Laughter and Forgetting*, translated from the French by Aaron Asher, London: Faber and Faber, 1996.
10 D. Sibley, *Geographies of Exclusion*, London: Routledge, 1995, p. 49.

8 Citizenship

1 T. Hall, A. Coffey and H. Williamson, 'Self, space and place: youth identities and citizenship', *British Journal of Sociology of Education*, 1999, vol. 20, no. 4, pp. 501–513.
2 J.S. Mill, *On Liberty*, London: Penguin, 1962.
3 J. Locke, *Locke: Political Essays*, ed. Mark Goldie, Cambridge: Cambridge University Press, 1997.
4 J-J. Rousseau, *The Social Contract*, trans. Maurice Cranston, Harmondsworth: Penguin, 1968.
5 T. Hobbes, *Leviathan*, London: Dent, 1914.
6 N.P. Berry, *An Introduction to Modern Political Theory* (3rd edn), London: Macmillan, 1995. Berry argues that 'much of liberal individualistic social theory is underpinned by a "fragmented" view of the person: a view that is well enough in relation to the explanation of the regularities of the market but is unsatisfactory elsewhere. This fragmentation of the person involves the detachment of agents from their social settings and treats them as rational choosers of utility maximisers', p. 22.
7 L. Doyal and L. Gough, *A Theory of Human Need*, Basingstoke: Macmillan, 1991.
8 I. Copeland, *The Making of the Backward Pupil in Education in England: 1870–1914*, London: Woburn Press, 1999, p. 135.
9 Royal Commission on the Blind, the Deaf and the Dumb, &c. of the United Kingdom, *Report*, London: HMSO, 1889, vol. 1, p. 95, quoted by Copeland, op. cit., p. 134.
10 Education Department, *Departmental Committee on Defective and Epileptic Children*, London: HMSO, 1898, quoted by Copeland, op. cit., p. 135.
11 Copeland, op. cit., p. 135. Copeland bases this conclusion on the findings of the Departmental Committee on Defective and Epileptic Children, which maintained that, 'The line that divides the dull or weak-minded man from the imbecile is the ability to earn a living . . . in the first degree of weakness of mind, the individual is able to earn his own livelihood. . . . The imbecile is unable to earn his own livelihood.' Ibid., pp. 134–135.
12 Ibid., pp. 2–3.
13 Ibid., p. 173. Source: Board of Education, *Statistics of Public Education in England and Wales, Education Statistics*, London: HMSO, 1900–1914.
14 D.G. Pritchard, *Education and the Handicapped 1760–1960*, London: Routledge and Kegan Paul, 1963, p. 188.
15 S. Tomlinson, *Educational Subnormality: A Study in Decision-Making*, London: Routledge and Kegan Paul, 1981, p. 81.
16 In education, this policy shows continuity from 1978 to 1997: Department of Education and Science, *Special Educational Needs* (The Warnock Report), London: HMSO, 1978; Department for Education and Employment, *Excellence for All Children: Meeting Special Educational Needs*, London: The Stationery Office, 1997. In respect of adults, this policy agenda is set out in policy guidelines issued by the Department of Health, *Community Care in the Next Decade and Beyond: Policy Guidelines*, London: HMSO, 1990.
17 P.M. Ferguson, D.L. Ferguson and S.J. Taylor (eds) *Interpreting Disability: A Qualitative Reader*, New York: Teachers College Press, 1992.
18 Department of Health, 'Virginia Bottomley opens conference on community care training', Press Release, London: DoH, 1991.
19 L. Dowse, 'Contesting practices, challenging codes: self-advocacy, disability politics and the social model of disability', *Disability and Society*, 2001, vol. 16, no. 1, pp. 123–141.

20 A pressure group – the 'Campaign for Mentally Handicapped People' – was formed in Britain and its first conference held in 1973. The 'People First' movement, which attempted to co-ordinate the international development of the self-advocacy movement, started at a planning conference in the USA in 1974. In 1984 a group of people with 'learning difficulties' set up 'People First in London', an organisation run by and for people with 'learning difficulties' and independent of all service provision. P. Williams and B. Shoultz, *We Can Speak for Ourselves*, London: Souvenir Press, 1982.
21 Ibid., p. 15.
22 Ibid., p. 16.
23 D. Goodley, *Self-advocacy in the Lives of People with Learning Difficulties: The Politics of Resilience*, Buckingham: Open University Press, 2000.
24 B. Crawley, *The Growing Voice: A Survey of Self-Advocacy Groups in Adult Training Centres and Hospitals in Great Britain*, London: Values Into Action, 1988.
25 S. Aspis, 'Self-advocacy for people with learning difficulties: does it have a future?' *Disability and Society*, 1997, vol. 12, no. 4, pp. 647–654: 652.
26 Ibid., p. 653.
27 M. Barnes and G. Wistow (eds) *Researching User Involvement*, Leeds: Nuffield Institute for Health, 1992.
28 S. Aspis, 'What they don't tell disabled people with learning difficulties', in M. Corker and S. French (eds) *Disability Discourse*, Buckingham: Open University Press, 1999, pp. 173–182: 182.
29 L. Barton, 'Insider perspectives, citizenship and the question of critical engagement', in M. Moore (ed.) *Insider Perspectives on Inclusion: Raising Voices, Raising Issues*, Sheffield: Philip Armstrong Publications, 2000, pp. 36–45: 40.

9 Seizing the future by recapturing the past

1 H-J. Striker, *A History of Disability*, trans. William Sayers, Ann Arbor, Mich.: University of Michigan Press, 1999, pp. 133–134.
2 S. Tomlinson, *Education in a Post-Welfare Society*, Buckingham: Open University Press, 2001.
3 Ibid., p. 99.
4 A. Marsh, *Funding Inclusive Education: The Economic Realities*, Aldershot: Ashgate, 2003.
5 Audit Commission, *Getting in on the Act. Provision for Pupils with Special Educational Needs: The National Picture*, London: HMSO, 1992. B. Norwich, *Segregation Statistics*, London: CSIE, 1994.
6 C. Cox, J. Douglas-Home, J. Marks, L. Norcross and R. Scruton, *Whose Schools?* London: The Hillgate Group, 1986. Tomlinson, op. cit. G. Whitty, 'The New Right and the National Curriculum: state control or market forces', *Journal of Educational Policy*, 1989, vol. 4, no. 4, pp. 329–342.
7 D. Galloway, D. Armstrong and S. Tomlinson, *The Assessment of Special Educational Needs. Whose Problem?* London: Longman, 1994.
8 The Office for Standards in Education (Ofsted) was established in 1992.
9 C. Benn and C. Chitty, *Thirty Years On: Is Comprehensive Education Alive and Well or Struggling to Survive?* London: David Fulton, 1996.
10 Ibid., p. 99.
11 Department for Education and Employment, *Excellence for All Children: Meeting Special Educational Needs*, London: The Stationery Office, 1997. Department for Education and Employment, *Meeting Special Educational Needs: A Programme for Action*, London: DfEE, 1998.

12 Department for Education and Employment, *Code of Practice on the Identification and Assessment of Special Educational Needs*, London: DfEE, 1994. Department for Education and Skills, *Special Educational Needs: Code of Practice*, London: DfES, 2001.
13 J. Young, *The Exclusive Society: Social Exclusion, Crime and Difference in Late Modernity*, London: Sage, 1999, p. 28.
14 D. Armstrong, *Power and Partnership in Education: Parents, Children and Special Educational Needs*, London: Routledge, 1995.
15 B. Coard, *How the West Indian Child is Made Educationally Sub-normal in the British School System*, London: New Beacon Books, 1971.
16 S. Tomlinson, *Educational Subnormality: A Study in Decision-Making*, London, Routledge and Kegan Paul, 1981.
17 In reply to a House of Commons question on the exclusion from school of black-Caribbean children, Baroness Ashton of Upholland reported that thirty-eight in every thousand, or 3 per cent, of primary and secondary school children permanently excluded from school were of black-Caribbean ethnic origin. House of Lords, 'School exclusions: pupils of black-Caribbean ethnic origin', *HL4560*, vol. 638, pt. 150, Wednesday, 12 June 2002.
18 For example, a quarter of Children Looked After were recorded in 'black' ethnic categories in 2001. Department of Health, 'Children in need: results of a survey of activity and expenditure by local authorities in England', Press Release, 22 February 2001.
19 In the year 2000 three thousand children served prison sentences. The number of black children incarcerated was over six times the average. J. Hyland, 'Children's Society, top prisons inspector call for end to jailing children in Britain, *World Socialist Web*, 28 November 2000. http://www.wsws.org/articles/2000/nov2000/pris-n28.shtml (accessed 15 December 2002).
20 D. Armstrong, D. Galloway and S. Tomlinson, 'Assessing special educational needs: the child's contribution', *British Educational Research Journal*, 1993, vol. 19, no. 2, pp. 119–129. D. Armstrong, 'Partnership with pupils: problems and possibilities', *Association for Child Psychologists and Psychiatrists, Occasional Papers* series, 2003, no. 20, pp. 39–45.
21 P. Freire, *The Politics of Education: Culture, Power and Liberation*, trans. D. Macedo, New York: Bergin & Garvey, 1985, p. 72.
22 Ibid., p. 73.
23 L. Barton, 'Inclusive education: romantic, subversive or realistic?' *International Journal of Inclusive Education*, 1997, vol. 1, no. 3, pp. 231–242: 234.

Bibliography

Aglietta, M., *A Theory of Capitalist Regulation*, London: New Left Books, 1979.

Armstrong, D., *Power and Partnership in Education: Parents, Children and Special Educational Needs*, London: Routledge, 1995.

—— *The Life Histories of People with Learning Difficulties* (Final Report to the Economic and Social Research Council, Grant No. R000221555), Swindon: ESRC, 1998.

—— 'The politics of self-advocacy and people with learning difficulties', *Policy and Politics*, 2002, vol. 30, no. 3, pp. 333–345.

—— 'Partnership with pupils: problems and possibilities', *Association for Child Psychologists and Psychiatrists, Occasional Papers* series, 2003, no. 20, pp. 39–45.

Armstrong, D. and Galloway, D., 'Who is the child psychologist's client? Responsibilities and options for psychologists in educational settings', *Association for Child Psychology and Psychiatry Newsletter*, 1992, vol. 14, no. 2, pp. 62–66.

—— 'On being a client: conflicting perspectives on assessment', in T. Booth, W. Swann, M. Masterton and P. Potts (eds) *Learning For All 2: Policies for Diversity in Education*, London: Routledge/Open University, 1992.

Armstrong, D., Galloway, D. and Tomlinson, S., 'Assessing special educational needs: the child's contribution', *British Educational Research Journal*, 1993, vol. 19, no. 2, pp. 119–129.

Armstrong, F., 'The historical development of special education: humanitarian rationality or "wild profusion of entangled events"?' *History of Education*, 2002, vol. 31, no. 5, pp. 437–450.

Aspis, S., 'Self-advocacy for people with learning difficulties: does it have a future?' *Disability and Society*, 1997, vol. 12, no. 4, pp. 647–654.

—— 'What they don't tell disabled people with learning difficulties', in M. Corker and S. French (eds) *Disability Discourse*, Buckingham: Open University Press, 1999, pp. 173–182.

Atkinson, D., Jackson, M. and Walmsley, J., *Forgotten Lives: Exploring the History of Learning Disability*, Plymouth: BILD, 1997.

Audit Commission, *Getting in on the Act. Provision for Pupils with Special Educational Needs: The National Picture*, London: HMSO, 1992.

Ball, S., *Education Reform: A Critical and Post-structural Approach*, Buckingham: Open University Press, 1994.

Barnes, M. and Wistow, G. (eds) *Researching User Involvement*, Leeds: Nuffield Institute for Health, 1992.

Barton, L., 'Inclusive education: romantic, subversive or realistic?' *International Journal of Inclusive Education*, 1997, vol. 1, no. 3, pp. 231–242: 234.

—— 'Insider perspectives, citizenship and the question of critical engagement', in M. Moore (ed.) *Insider Perspectives on Inclusion: Raising Voices, Raising Issues*, Sheffield: Philip Armstrong Publications, 2000, pp. 36–45.

Bauman, Z., *Thinking Sociologically*, Oxford: Blackwell, 1990.

Beck, U., *Risk Society: Towards a New Modernity*, trans. Mark Ritter, London: Sage, 1992.

Becker, H.S., *The Outsiders: Case Studies in the Sociology of Deviance*, New York: The Free Press, 1963.

Benn, C. and Chitty, C., *Thirty Years On: Is Comprehensive Education Alive and Well or Struggling to Survive?* London: David Fulton, 1996.

Berry, N.P., *An Introduction to Modern Political Theory* (3rd edn), London: Macmillan, 1995.

Best, S. and Kellner, D., *Postmodern Theory: Critical Interrogations*, New York: Guilford Press, 1991.

Bhaskar, R., *Philosophy and the Human Sciences: A Philosophical Critique of the Contemporary Human Sciences, Vol. 1 The Possibility of Naturalism*, Brighton: Harvester Press, 1979.

Blumer, H., 'Society as symbolic interaction', in A.M. Rose (ed.) *Human Behavior and Social Processes*, Boston: Houghton Mifflin, 1962.

—— *Symbolic Interactionism*, Englewood Cliffs: Prentice-Hall, 1969.

Board of Education, *Statistics of Public Education in England and Wales, Education Statistics*, London: HMSO, 1900–1914.

—— *Report of the Mental Deficiency Committee* (The Wood Committee), London: Board of Education, 1929.

Booth, T., 'Challenging conceptions of integration', in L. Barton (ed.) *The Politics of Special Educational Needs*, London: Falmer Press, 1988.

—— 'Inclusion and exclusion in England: who controls the agenda?' in F. Armstrong, D. Armstrong and L. Barton (eds) *Inclusive Education: Policy, Contexts and Comparative Perspectives*, London: David Fulton, 2000.

Bottomore, T. and Rubel, M., *Karl Marx: Selected Writings in Sociology and Social Philosophy*, London: Penguin, 1963.

Brennan, W., *Curricular Needs for Slow Learners*, London: Evans, 1979.

Callaghan, J., 'Speech by the Prime Minister, the Rt. Hon. James Callaghan, MP, at a foundation-stone laying ceremony at Ruskin College, Oxford, on 18th October', Press Release, 1976.

Carr, E.H., *What Is History?* London: Penguin, 1964.

Central Advisory Council for Education (CASE), *Children and their Primary Schools* (The Plowden Report), London: HMSO, 1967.

Charon, J.M., *Symbolic Interactionism: An Introduction, an Interpretation, an Integration*, Englewood Cliffs: Prentice-Hall, 1979.

Cicourel, A. and Kitsuse, J., *The Educational Decision-Makers*, Indianapolis: Bobbs Merrill, 1963.

Coard, B., *How the West Indian Child is Made Educationally Sub-normal in the British School System*, London: New Beacon Books, 1971.

Coffey, A., *Education and Social Change*, Buckingham: Open University Press, 2001.

Coffield, F., 'Introduction and overview: attempts to reclaim the concept of the learning society', *Journal of Educational Policy*, 1997, vol. 12, no. 6, pp. 449–455.

Collingwood, R.G., *The Idea of History*, London: Oxford University Press, 1961.

Compton, E., *A History of Whittington Parish*, Leeds: The Standard Publishing Company, 1931.

Copeland, I., *The Making of the Backward Pupil in Education in England: 1870–1914*, London: Woburn Press, 1999.

—— 'Pragmatism: past examples concerning pupils with learning difficulties', *History of Education*, 2001, vol. 30, no. 1, pp. 1–12.

Cox, C., Douglas-Home, J., Marks, J., Norcross, L. and Scruton, R., *Whose Schools?* London: The Hillgate Group, 1986.

Crawley, B., *The Growing Voice: A Survey of Self-Advocacy Groups in Adult Training Centres and Hospitals in Great Britain*, London: Values Into Action, 1988.

Culpitt, I., *Social Policy and Risk*, London: Sage, 1999.

Dale, R., *The State and Education Policy*, Milton Keynes: Open University Press, 1989.

Department for Education, *Choice and Diversity: A New Framework for Schools*, Cmnd 2021, London: HMSO, 1992.

Department for Education and Employment, *Code of Practice on the Identification and Assessment of Special Educational Needs*, London: DfEE, 1994.

—— *Excellence for All Children: Meeting Special Educational Needs*, London: The Stationery Office, 1997.

—— *Meeting Special Educational Needs: A Programme for Action*, London: DfEE, 1998.

Department for Education and Skills, *Special Educational Needs: Code of Practice*, London: DfES, 2001.

Department of Education and Science, 'The last to come in', *Report on Education, no. 69*, London: HMSO, 1971.

—— *Special Educational Needs* (The Warnock Report), London: HMSO, 1978.

Department of Health, *Community Care in the Next Decade and Beyond: Policy Guidelines*, London: HMSO, 1990.

—— 'Virginia Bottomley opens conference on community care training', Press Release, London: DoH, 1991.

—— 'Children in need: results of a survey of activity and expenditure by local authorities in England', Press Release, 22 February 2001.

Derbyshire Times, 'School visit of Lady Mackintosh', 3 November 1923.

Dewey, J., *Philosophy, Psychology and Social Practice – Selected Essays*, New York: G.P. Putnam's Sons, 1963.

Digby, A. and Wright, D., *From Idiocy to Mental Deficiency: Historical Perspectives on People with Learning Difficulties*, London: Routledge, 1996.

Dowse, L., 'Contesting practices, challenging codes: self-advocacy, disability politics and the social model of disability', *Disability and Society*, 2001, vol. 16, no. 1, pp. 123–141.

Doyal, L. and Gough, L., *A Theory of Human Need*, Basingstoke: Macmillan, 1991.

Duncan, J., *Mental Deficiency*, London: Watts & Co, 1938.
Education Department, *Departmental Committee on Defective and Epileptic Children*, London: HMSO, 1898.
Ferguson, P.M., Ferguson, D.L. and Taylor, S.J. (eds) *Interpreting Disability: A Qualitative Reader*, New York: Teachers College Press, 1992.
Finch, J., *Education as Social Policy*, London: Longman, 1984.
Ford, J., Mongon, D. and Whelan, M., *Special Education and Social Control: Invisible Disasters*, London: Routledge and Kegan Paul, 1982.
Foucault, M., *Madness and Civilization: A History of Insanity in the Age of Reason*, London: Tavistock, 1967.
—— *The Archaeology of Knowledge*, London: Tavistock, 1972.
—— *Discipline and Punish: The Birth of the Prison*, London: Peregrine Books, 1979.
Franklin, B.M., *From 'Backwardness' to 'At Risk': Childhood Learning Difficulties and the Contradictions of School Reform*, Albany: State University of New York Press, 1994.
Freire, P., *The Politics of Education: Culture, Power and Liberation*, trans. D. Macedo, New York: Bergin & Garvey, 1985.
Fulcher, G., *Disabling Policies: A Comparative Approach to Educational Policy and Disability*, Lewes: Falmer Press, 1989.
Galloway, D., *Schools, Pupils and Special Educational Needs*, London: Croom Helm, 1985.
Galloway, D. and Goodwin, C., *The Education of Disturbing Children*, London: Longman, 1987.
Galloway, D., Armstrong, D. and Tomlinson, S., *The Assessment of Special Educational Needs. Whose Problem?* London: Longman, 1994.
Galton, F., *Hereditary Genius, its Laws and Consequences*, London: Macmillan, 1869.
Giddens, A., *Social Theory and Modern Sociology*, Cambridge: Polity Press, 1987.
Giroux, H., *Theory and Resistance in Education: A Pedagogy for the Opposition*, London: Heinemann, 1983.
Goddard, H.H., *Feeble-Mindedness: Its Causes and Consequences*, New York: Macmillan, 1914.
Goffman, E., *Asylums: Essays on the Social Situation of Mental Patients and Other Inmates*, London: Pelican, 1968.
Goldthorpe, J., Lockwood, D., Beckhefer, F. and Platt, J., *The Affluent Worker in the Class Structure*, Cambridge: Cambridge University Press, 1968.
Goodley, D., *Self-advocacy in the Lives of People with Learning Difficulties: The Politics of Resilience*, Buckingham: Open University Press, 2000.
Goodson, I. and Sikes, P., *Life History Research in Educational Settings: Learning from Lives*, Buckingham: Open University Press, 2001.
Gramsci, A., *Selections from the Prison Notebooks*, London: Lawrence and Wishart, 1971.
Habermas, J., *The Theory of Communicative Action: Vol. 1 Reason and the Rationalization of Society*, Boston: Beacon Press, 1984.
—— *The Theory of Communicative Action: Vol. 2 Lifeworld and System*, Boston: Beacon Press, 1987.

Hall, T., Coffey, A. and Williamson, H., 'Self, space and place: youth identities and citizenship', *British Journal of Sociology of Education*, 1999, vol. 20, no. 4, pp. 501–513.

Hammersley, M., *Reading Ethnographic Research: A Critical Guide*, New York: Routledge, 1998.

Hargreaves, A., 'Revisiting voice', *Educational Researcher*, 1996, vol. 25, no. 1, pp. 12–19.

Harvey, D., *The Condition of Postmodernity: An Enquiry into the Origins of Cultural Change*, Oxford: Blackwell, 1990.

Hearnshaw, L.S., *Cyril Burt: Psychologist*, London: Hodder and Stoughton, 1979.

Hobbes, T., *Leviathan*, London: Dent, 1914.

House of Lords, 'School exclusions: pupils of black-Caribbean ethnic origin', *HL4560*, vol. 638, pt. 150, Wednesday, 12 June 2002.

Humphries, S. and Gordon, P., *Out of Sight*, London: Northcote House, 1992.

Hurt, J., *Outside the Mainstream: A History of Special Education*, London: Routledge, 1988.

Hyland, J., 'Children's Society, top prisons inspector call for end to jailing children in Britain, *World Socialist Web*, 28 November 2000. http://www.wsws.org/articles/2000/nov2000/pris-n28.shtml (accessed 15 December 2002).

Ireland, W.W., *On Idiocy and Imbecility*, London: J. & A. Churchill, 1877.

Kemshall, H., *Risk, Social Policy and Welfare*, Buckingham: Open University Press, 2002.

Kenworthy, J. and Whittaker, J., 'Anything to declare? The struggle for inclusive education and children's rights', *Disability and Society*, 2000, vol. 15, pp. 219–231.

Kincheloe, J., 'Educational historiographical meta analysis: rethinking methodology in the 1990s', *International Journal of Qualitative Studies in Education*, 1992, vol. 4, no. 3, pp. 231–245.

Kirp, D.L., 'Professionalism as a policy choice: British special education in comparative perspective', in J.B. Chambers and W.T. Hartman (eds) *Special Education Policies: Their History, Implementation and Finance*, Philadelphia: Temple University Press, 1983.

Kundera, M., *The Book of Laughter and Forgetting*, trans. from the French by Aaron Asher, London: Faber and Faber, 1996.

Lather, P., *Getting Smart: Feminist Research and Pedagogy within the Postmodern*, New York: Routledge, 1991.

—— 'Fertile obsession: validity after poststructuralism', in A. Gitlin (ed.) *Power and Method: Political Activism and Educational Research*, New York: Routledge, 1994.

Lipsky, M., *Street-level Bureaucracy: Dilemmas of the Individual in Public Service*, New York: Russell Sage Foundation, 1980.

Locke, J., *Locke: Political Essays*, ed. Mark Goldie, Cambridge: Cambridge University Press, 1997.

Lupton, D. (ed.) *Risk and Sociocultural Theory: New Directions and Perspectives*, Cambridge: Cambridge University Press, 1999.

McClaren, P., *Critical Pedagogy and Predatory Culture: Oppositional Politics in a Postmodern Era*, London: Routledge, 1995.

McCulloch, G., *Educational Reconstruction: The 1944 Education Act and the Twenty-First Century*, Ilford: Woburn Press, 1994.

—— *Failing the Ordinary Child? The Theory and Practice of Working-Class Secondary Education*, Buckingham: Open University Press, 1998.

—— 'Representing the "ordinary child": the case of the Newsome Committee, 1961–1963', *Journal of Educational Administration and History*, 2000, vol. 32, no. 1, pp. 51–65.

McCulloch, G. and Richardson, W., *Historical Research in Educational Settings*, Buckingham: Open University Press, 2000.

Marsh, A., *Funding Inclusive Education: The Economic Realities*, Aldershot: Ashgate, 2003.

Marx, K., 'The German Ideology', in K. Marx and F. Engels, *Collected Works*, vol. 5, London: Lawrence and Wishart, 1976.

May, T., *Reconsidering Difference*, University Park, Pa.: Pennsylvania State University Press, 1997.

Mead, G.H., *Mind, Self and Society*, Chicago: Chicago University Press, 1934.

Middleton, S., *Educating Feminists: Life Histories and Pedagogy*, New York: Teachers College Press, 1993.

Mill, J.S., *On Liberty*, London: Penguin, 1962.

Mills, C.W., *The Sociological Imagination*, London: Oxford University Press, 1959.

Ministry of Education, *Handicapped Pupils and School Health Regulations*, Statutory Rules and Orders, no. 1076, London: HMSO, 1945.

—— *Handicapped Pupils and School Health Regulations*, Statutory Instruments, no. 365, London: HMSO, 1959.

Moore, R. and Muller, J., 'The discourse of "voice" and the problem of knowledge and identity in the sociology of education', *British Journal of Sociology of Education*, 1999, vol. 20, no. 2, pp. 189–205.

Morris, P., *Put Away*, London: Routledge and Kegan Paul, 1969.

Murray, P., 'Living with the spark: recognising ordinariness in the lives of disabled children and their families', PhD thesis, University of Sheffield, 2003.

Nietzsche, F., *The Will to Power*, New York: Vintage Books, 1968.

Norwich, B., *Segregation Statistics*, London: CSIE, 1994.

Oakeshott, M., *Experience and its Modes*, Cambridge: Cambridge University Press, 1933.

Okely, J., *Own or Other Culture*, London: Routledge, 1996.

Oswin, M., 'A historical perspective', in C. Robinson and K. Stalker (eds) *Growing Up With Disability*, London: Jessica Kingsley Publications, 1998.

Pareto, V., *Sociological Writings*, ed. S.E. Finer, London: Pall Mall, 1966.

Popkewitz, T.S., Franklin, B.M. and Pereyra, M.A.,'Preface', in T.S. Popkewitz, M.A. Pereyra and B.M. Franklin (eds) *Cultural History and Education: Critical Essays on Knowledge and Schooling*, New York: RoutledgeFalmer, 2001.

Popkewitz, T.S., Pereyra, M.A. and Franklin, B.M., 'History, the problem of knowledge, and the new cultural histories of schooling', in T.S. Popkewitz *et al.* (eds) op. cit., 2001.

Porter, R., *A Social History of Madness: Stories of the Insane*, London: Phoenix, 1996.

Pritchard, D.G., *Education and the Handicapped 1760-1960*, London: Routledge and Kegan Paul, 1963.

Reiser, R., 'Disabled history or a history of the disabled', in M. Mason and R. Reiser (eds) *Disability Equality in the Classroom – A Human Rights Issue*, London: Inner London Education Authority, 1990.

Riddell, S., Baron, S., Stalker, K. and Wilkinson, H., 'The concept of the learning society for adults with learning difficulties: human and social capital perspectives', *Journal of Educational Policy*, 1997, vol. 12, no. 6, pp. 473–484.

Rorty, R., *Philosophy and the Mirror of Nature*, Princeton: Princeton University Press, 1979.

Rousseau, J-J., *The Social Contract*, trans. Maurice Cranston, Harmondsworth: Penguin, 1968.

Royal Commission on the Blind, the Deaf and the Dumb, &c. of the United Kingdom, *Report*, London: HMSO, 1889.

Royal Commission on Elementary Education Acts, *Final Report* (The Cross Commission), London: HMSO, 1888.

Rutter, S. and Sayman, S., *'He'll Never Join the Army': A Report on a Down's Syndrome Association Survey into Attitudes to People with Down's Syndrome Amongst Medical Professionals*, London: Down's Syndrome Association, 1999.

Rutter, M., Maughn, B., Mortimore, P., Ouston, J. and Smith, A., *Fifteen Thousand Hours: Secondary Schools and their Effects on Pupils*, London: Open Books, 1979.

Ryan, J. and Thomas, F., *The Politics of Mental Handicap*, London: Free Association Books, 1987.

Sartre, J-P., *Being and Nothingness*, London: Routledge, 1989.

Scott, J., *Dominion and the Arts of Resistance: Hidden Transcripts*, New Haven, Conn.: Yale University Press, 1990.

Sibley, D., *Geographies of Exclusion*, London: Routledge, 1995.

Silver, H., *Education as History: Interpreting Nineteenth and Twentieth Century History*, London: Methuen, 1983.

Sparkes, A.C., 'Life histories and the issue of voice: reflections on an emerging relationship', *Qualitative Studies in Education*, 1994, vol. 7, no. 2, pp. 165–183.

Stone, D., *The Disabled State*, Basingstoke: Macmillan, 1984.

Striker, H-J., *A History of Disability*, trans. William Sayers, Ann Arbor, Mich.: University of Michigan Press, 1999.

Sutherland, G., *Ability, Merit and Measurement: Mental Testing and English Education 1880–1940*, Oxford: Clarendon Press, 1984.

Tawney, R.H., *Equality* (4th edn), London: George Allen and Unwin, 1952.

Thompson, E.P., *The Making of the English Working Class*, London: Gollancz, 1963.

Tomlinson, S., *Educational Subnormality: A Study in Decision-Making*, London: Routledge and Kegan Paul, 1981.

—— *A Sociology of Special Education*, London: Routledge and Kegan Paul, 1982.

—— 'The expansion of special education', *Oxford Review of Education*, 1985, vol. 11, no. 2, pp. 157–165.

—— 'Why Johnny can't read: critical theory and special education', *European Journal of Special Needs Education*, 1988, vol. 3, pp. 45–58.

—— 'The expansion of special education', in B. Cosin, M. Flude and M. Hales (eds) *School, Work and Equality*, Sevenoaks: Hodder, 1989.

—— *Education in a Post-Welfare Society*, Buckingham: Open University Press, 2001.

Tredgold, A., 'The feeble-minded: a social danger', *Eugenics Review*, 1909, vol. 1, pp. 97–104.

Tutt, N., 'The unintended consequences of integration', *Educational and Child Psychology*, 1985, vol. 2, no. 3, pp. 130–138.

UNICEF, *The Convention on the Rights of the Child*, London: United Kingdom Committee for UNICEF, 1995.

Whitty, G., 'The New Right and the National Curriculum: state control or market forces', *Journal of Educational Policy*, 1989, vol. 4, no. 4, pp. 329–342.

Whyte, W.F., *Street Corner Society: The Social Structure of an Italian Slum* (3rd edn), Chicago: Chicago University Press, 1981.

Williams, P. and Shoultz, B., *We Can Speak for Ourselves*, London: Souvenir Press, 1982.

Young, J., *The Exclusive Society: Social Exclusion, Crime and Difference in Late Modernity*, London: Sage, 1999.

Index